$\equiv$ **50 YEARS** $\equiv$
OF
YANKEE
A L L - S T A R S

50 YEARS
OF
YANKEE
ALL - STARS

Mark Gallagher

LEISURE PRESS

A publication of
Leisure Press
597 Fifth Avenue, New York, NY 10017

Library of Congress Cataloging in Publication Data

Gallagher, Mark.

50 years of Yankee all-stars.

1. Baseball players—United States—Biography.
2. New York Yankees (Baseball team) I. Title. II. Title:
Fifty years of Yankee all-stars.
GV865.A1G34 1984 796.357'092'02 [B] 84-2907
ISBN 0-88011-161-5

CONTENTS

INTRODUCTION

The first All-Star Game was an adjunct to a world's fair. It was an exhibition of big league greats at Chicago's Century of Progress Exposition.

The prime mover behind the game, played July 6, 1933, at Comiskey Park, was Arch Ward, sports editor of the *Chicago Tribune*. He persuaded Baseball Commissioner Kenesaw Mountain Landis that an exhibition by the stars of the game would be great for baseball. And it was. The gate was great, too—47,595 attended—and the All-Star Game became an annual event.

Arch Ward started something good. His was a great idea, and he stayed with it. But it was not a novel idea. Exhibitions by assembled major league stars had been held prior to 1933. For example, a few months after the 1911 death of Cleveland's great pitcher, Addie Joss, a team of American League All-Stars played the Indians in a benefit game for Joss' widow. On the All-Star squad were New York's Hal Chase, the fancy first baseman, and pitcher Russ Ford.

Gather your team's All-Stars and you've assembled your team's greats, you could say. Unfortunately, this doesn't quite work. Because the Yankees date back to 1903, thirty years of Yankees never had a shot at becoming All-Stars. These greats include not only the aforementioned Chase and Ford, but such prominent players as Jack Chesbro, Earle Combs, Waite Hoyt, Willie Keeler, Bob Meusel, Roger Peckinpaugh, Herb Pennock, Wally Pipp, Wally Schang, and Bob Shawkey. Each of these players would have been good for at least one All-Star appearance.

Ward wanted the fans to select the All-Star squads, and the fans did make the selections, with the managers rounding out the team rosters. But in 1935 the managers began choosing the players, starters included. And they did so until 1947, when the selection process reverted to the fans, who chose their All-Stars (pitchers excepted) by nationwide poll. But the fans lost the vote after ballot stuffings in Cincinnati, and the eight starters were picked by managers, coaches, and players. Selection worked this way from 1958 until 1970, when Commissioner Bowie Kuhn returned the selection of each league's eight starters to the fans.

Whatever the decision-making mechanics, the fans are the final arbiter. In an effort to raise more money for the players' pension fund, big league baseball put on two All-Star Games per year from 1959 through 1962. But the fans saw this as one game too many and forced a return to the single-game format.

To the 50 Summer Classics that have been held since the first official All-Star Game, the New York Yankees have contributed 80 players. The purpose of this book is to convey the sense of the greatness of each of these outstanding athletes.

Connie Mack of the American League and John McGraw of the National League were the first All-Star managers. Thereafter, the managers of the previous year's pennant winners usually have been given the honor of managing their respective league's All-Stars. Yankee managers who have led the Americans into battle are Joe McCarthy (seven games); Bucky Harris (one); Casey Stengel (10); Ralph Houk (three); Billy Martin (two); and Bob Lemon (one). Only McCarthy and Harris hold winning records.

Yankee All-Star players have included Babe Ruth, Lou Gehrig, Joe DiMaggio and Mickey Mantle, players for whom the term "Superstar" may be more fitting. A galaxy of 80 stars, some even brighter than others, but all Stars—the best of a half century of Yankee baseball. Presented here along with profiles of the 80 Yankee All-Stars are "New York Yankee All-Star Game Highlights"—a game-by-game account of key Yankee roles and actions over 50 years of All-Star competition. The author wishes to thank those who assisted in the preparation of this book, especially the New York Yankees in the person of David Szen.

Every book has a time perspective; the look-back point for this book is the summer of 1983—the 50th anniversary of the All-Star Game.

PLAYERS' BIOGRAPHIES

LUIS ARROYO

Career
The Yankees purchased the contract of Luis Arroyo, former National Leaguer, in the summer of 1960 when Arroyo was toiling for Jersey City, a Cincinnati farm club. Luis' four-season record in the senior circuit was an unimpressive 18–22. And he was 33. The Yankees put him on the firing line and he went 5–1 with seven saves in 29 relief appearances in 1960.

A dream season came true for Luis in 1961. He led the league in games pitched, relief wins, and saves. His 65 game appearances established a Yankee record that stood for 13 years. He had 15 relief wins (against only five losses) and 29 saves. In other words, he had a hand in 44 of New York's 109 victories! The affable, 5'8" cigar-smoking, screwball artist from Puerto Rico won a league-record 12 consecutive games in relief. He also won Fireman of the Year honors and a key game over Cincinnati in the World Series.

Unfortunately, Arroyo's magic faded quickly. A lame arm put him on the disabled list in May of 1962 and he was never the same after that.

All-Star
The majors played two All-Star Games in 1961. Luis Arroyo was added to the roster for the second game, played in Boston's Fenway Park. Luis didn't pitch; the American League worked only righties in the game that ended in a 1–1 tie.

Yankee Stats
	W	L	PCT	G	GS	CG	SA	SO	ERA
4 Years	22	10	.688	127	0	0	43	142	3.12
2 World Series	1	0	1.000	3	0	0	0	4	3.86
All-Star Games (no appearances)									

LUIS ARROYO (NY Yankees)

HANK BAUER

HANK BAUER

Career

Hank Bauer holds one of the most incredible—and least known—records in baseball: He hit safely in 17 consecutive games in World Series competition. Bauer made at least one hit in each contest of the seven-game 1956 Series. Ditto for the seven-game 1957 Series. He then hit safely in the first three games of the 1958 Series (Warren Spahn snapped the streak in Game 4). Outstanding performances in pressure situations made Bauer one of the top players of his era.

It was a long winding road to the majors for Bauer. The native of East St. Louis, Illinois, was 26 when he reached the Yankees late in the summer of 1948, his career having been interrupted by four war years with the marines. In 19 New York games over the final weeks of 1948, Hank hit only .180.

Bauer's career blossomed under Casey Stengel, who became Yankee manager in 1949. The pair's Yankee careers were almost simultaneous, with Hank helping win nine of Stengel's 10 pennants. In their early years together, Stengel often platooned Bauer in the outfield (Hank had only 301 at bats in 1949), but thereafter Bauer had only three Yankee seasons of fewer than 400 at bats. Bauer became a regular and complete player who could run, field, and hit.

Inside Bauer burned an unquenchable desire to win. A World Series check was important to him and he refused to let anyone needlessly deny him the extra pay. "Don't mess with my money," Bauer would tell a loafing teammate. He was a natural leader and he led by example. Bauer, known as "Bruiser," played hardnosed ball, always put out 100 percent, and never quit. But he was a clean player, a man with a profound sense of fairness on and off the field.

Right-handed power hitters at Yankee Stadium are at a distinct disadvantage. Yet Bauer hit 158 home runs as a Yankee. Only four other right-handed Yankees have hit more. He often batted first in the order and over his career he hit 18 leadoff homers, ranking him with baseball's all-time leaders. In 1956, his best season for power, Hank hit 26 homers with 84 RBIs and 96 runs scored. In the 1958 World Series, he launched four home runs.

Bauer's .277 lifetime average is not too shabby, either. His career high was .320 in 1950; over the combined five seasons from 1950 through 1954 he hit .301 (642 for 2,130). In the 1955 World Series, Hank batted .429.

But like Lou Piniella of today's Yanks, Bauer's statistics fail to register his real worth. Casey Stengel once said about Bauer, "Too many people judge ballplayers solely by a hundred runs batted in or a .300 batting average. I like to judge my players in other ways. Like the guy who happens to do everything right in a tough situation." One such tough situation was the final game of the 1951 World Series against the Giants, which the Yankees won, 4–3. All Bauer did was hit a bases-loaded triple and, with two out in the ninth, save the game by making a sliding catch in right field of Sal Yvars' liner as the would-be tying run scampered home.

The Yankees traded Bauer to the Kansas City A's in December 1959 as part of the deal that brought Roger Maris to New York. Bauer went on to manage three American League clubs and lead the Orioles to the 1966 World Championship. His much-lauded successor, Earl Weaver, could do no more than tie Bauer in the number of World Championships brought to Baltimore. When it comes to winning, few in baseball have topped Bauer's dedication to the cause.

All-Star

Hank Bauer was a starter on the American League's All-Star teams in 1952, 1953, and 1954, playing in right field. He went 2-for-7 at the plate overall and was honored in the 1953 game when he batted third in a power-laden lineup. Others in the lineup included home run and RBI champ Al Rosen, batting champ Mickey Vernon, Yogi Berra, and Gus Zernial. Mickey Mantle batted fourth.

Yankee Stats

	G	AB	R	H	2B	3B	HR	RBI	BA
12 Years	1,406	4,784	792	1,326	211	56	158	654	.277
9 World Series	53	188	21	46	2	3	7	24	.245
All-Star Games	3	7	0	2	0	0	0	0	.286

YOGI BERRA

Career

Born in St. Louis on May 12, 1925, Lawrence Peter Berra, to be known to millions of Americans as Yogi, played 18 seasons for the New York Yankees (1946–63). He enjoyed a great career, winning three MVP awards and a place in the Baseball Hall of Fame.

Having signed for a $500 bonus, Berra began playing in the Yankee farm system in 1943. He spent two World War II years in the navy, then returned in 1946 to hit .314 at Newark. Yogi was called up to New York late in the 1946 season and went 8-for-22; two of his hits were homers. Yankee President Larry MacPhail—who couldn't believe the squatty Berra was actually a ballplayer when he first saw him—watched with pride as the improbable Yogi performed capably and promised more than competence.

No one ever questioned Berra's ability to hit. After all, there was that doubleheader day when he collected 21 RBIs while playing for Norfolk. ("There were a lot of men on base," Yogi explained.) But finding a place in the field where Yogi would do the least damage posed a problem. He was awkward and unpolished as a catcher, and he often played outfield in his early career. In the spring of 1949, Casey Stengel made Berra's advancement as a catcher a top priority. Bill Dickey was given the task of teaching Yogi the tricks of the trade. The lessons from Dickey paid off handsomely. Within a few years, Berra was the best defensive catcher in baseball.

Yogi was New York's regular catcher from 1949 through 1959. Yes, he was thick and stocky. But he was strong, quick, and amazingly fast over short distances. He is one of nine major league catchers to record a pair of unassisted double plays in his career—Yogi's coming 15 years apart! His strong arm helped him take part in 175 double plays; in the history of the league, only Ray Schalk has chalked up more. Yogi was sure-handed, which is evidenced by his incredible streak of 148 straight errorless games between July 1957 and May 1959, a major league record for a catcher.

Berra was durable, dependable, and tireless, and he understood the psychology of catching, of calling pitches, and of handling pitchers. For eight years in a row (1950–57), Yogi led the league in most games caught. The first game Yogi caught in 1962 was a 22-inning marathon with the Tigers; the 37-year-old Yogi went the distance. Once Berra began calling pitches in the early 1950s, he made it one

YOGI BERRA (NY Yankees)

of the strong suits of his game. He simply had the knack and intelligence to consistently outguess batters. He caught three no-hitters (only Schalk caught more) and he knew how to get the most out of his pitchers. With a fierce veteran like Vic Raschi, Yogi would goad and evoke that fighting response. But with a young pitcher who needed gentler handling, Yogi acted accordingly. No catcher ever handled pitchers better than Yogi did.

But Yogi is best remembered as the hitter who time after time came through in the clutch. In a tight situation with Berra at bat at Yankee Stadium, an opposing pitcher could feel the right field porch beckoning behind him. Yogi had few peers as a power hitter. He hit 313 lifetime home runs as a catcher, the most in league history, and his 30 homers in both 1952 and 1956 stood as the single-season league mark for catchers until Lance Parrish topped it with 32 homers in 1982.

Berra was *the* run-producer on the Yankees from the last few years of Joe DiMaggio's career until the full blossoming of Mickey Mantle. In each of seven seasons from 1949 through 1955, he led the club in RBIs. Yogi went 11 seasons in a row in which he delivered at least 82 RBIs, including five seasons of 100-plus RBIs, a remarkable achievement, especially for a catcher.

Yogi was known as one of the game's greatest bad-ball hitters. He was aggressive and swung at anything that looked good. And most pitches looked good. On striking out after once being asked to give a little more thought at the plate, Yogi pleaded, "How can I hit and think at the same time?" It was but one in a string of Yogi-isms.

Strangely and humorously phrased, Yogi's Yogi-isms were usually sensible, too. He once complained of bat "chipping," bringing a representative of Hillerich and Bradsby, the bat company, to New York to investigate. Berra was holding the bat improperly, with the trademark "up," the company man determined. "I go up there to swing, not to read," countered Yogi.

That was Yogi. But he was no joke. He built a fine life for his family through his baseball earnings, which he invested soundly. The Squire of Montclair, New Jersey, and his wife reared three athletic sons, all of whom entered professional sports.

As a 38-year-old player-coach in 1963, Berra hit .293, eight points higher than his lifetime average. The next year he managed the Yankees to a come-from-behind pennant. After being unfairly re-leased, Berra went over to the Mets to join Stengel. In 1973, Berra piloted the Mets to a pennant and became the second manager in history (behind Joe McCarthy) to win a flag in each major league.

Luckily, Yogi rejoined the Yankees a couple of years later as a coach under Billy Martin.

Yogi was an October fixture in the 1950s. He hit the first pinch-hit homer and the fifth grand slam homer in World Series history. After some rough Octobers early in his career, Yogi hit .429 in the 1953 Series, .417 in the 1955 Series, .360 in the 1956 Series and .320 in the 1957 Series. Sustained clutch hitting, indeed. Berra's name is etched in World Series records. He made more hits than anyone in Series history (71) and threw out more base stealers (36). He played in more Series (14) and on more Series winners (10) than anyone else.

All-Star

In his 18 years with the Yankees, Yogi Berra was picked to the American League's All-Star team in 15 seasons, making the team in every season from 1948 to 1962. After sitting out the 1948 game (Buddy Rosar and Birdie Tebbetts did the catching), Berra missed only the first game in 1959, the second game in 1961, and the first game in 1962. All told, Yogi played in 15 Summer Classics (including two in 1960) and at bat went a combined 8-for-41, as a catcher and pinch-hitter. Berra set All-Star Game records as a catcher for most games played behind the plate (14), putouts (61), assists (7) and total chances accepted (68).

He had several fine performances in All-Star Games. He made two hits and scored twice in the 1954 game, caught all 12 innings in the 1955 game, batted 2-for-2 in the 1956 game, and hit a long two-run homer off Don Drysdale at the Los Angeles Coliseum in the second 1959 game. Yogi was made honorary captain of the American League team in 1982, but not even Yogi's inspiration could keep the junior circuit from losing.

Yankee Stats

	G	AB	R	H	2B	3B	HR	RBI	BA
18 Years	2,116	7,546	1,174	2,148	321	49	358	1,430	.285
14 World Series	75	259	41	71	10	0	12	39	.274
All-Star Games	15	41	5	8	0	0	1	3	.195

BOBBY BONDS

Career

Long and lean Bobby Bonds combined raw power with a thorough-bred's speed and grace. He emulated his former San Francisco teammate, Willie Mays, but some felt Bonds was the more naturally talented of the two.

Bonds came to the Yankees from the Giants in 1974 for Bobby Murcer. A Californian, he was uncomfortable in the Big Apple, and he was hampered by a serious knee injury. Yet, the right fielder had a fine 1975 season, hitting 32 homers and stealing 30 bases. Over his career, Bonds had five 30-homer/30-stolen-base seasons; Mays is the only other player to have more than one such season, and he had two. However, Bonds struck out 137 times, breaking Mickey Mantle's club record of 126. (Bonds had set a big league record in 1969 with 187 strikeouts, a record he broke the following year with 189.) The Yankees traded Bonds to the Angels following the 1975 season.

All-Star

The American League in the 1975 All-Star Game started Bobby Bonds, Joe Rudi, and Reggie Jackson in the outfield. Bobby played center field in the absence of a natural center fielder and nailed a runner trying for one base too many. He was hitless in three trips.

Yankee Stats

	G	AB	R	H	2B	3B	HR	RBI	BA
1 Year	145	529	93	143	26	3	32	85	.270
All-Star Games	1	3	0	0	0	0	0	0	.000

BOBBY BONDS

Career

The Yankee braintrust in the spring of 1940 made an uncharacteristic mistake that probably cost a pennant. The mistake was to give 27-year-old Ernie Bonham another year in the minors. Recalled in August, Bonham went 9–3, completed 10 of 12 starts, and posted a 1.90 ERA over the final two months. But it was not enough to keep a Yankee miracle run from falling two games short.

Born in Ione, California, Bonham earned the nickname "Tiny" by growing to 215 pounds. As a Yank, he was a solid pitcher on the deep staffs of Joe McCarthy's reign. He was a control pitcher, walking only 1.67 batters per nine innings over his career to rank among the game's all-time leaders in this statistic. Of former Yankees who pitched at least 800 innings, only Russ Ford, Jack Chesbro, and Al Orth have earned run averages as Yankees that fall below Ernie's 2.73.

Bonham had his greatest campaign in 1942. He went 21–5 and joined Boston's Tex Hughson (22–6) as the league's only 20-game winners. (Ernie pitched in only 28 games; Tex took part in 38.) Bonham led the league in complete games (22) and shutouts (6), and his winning percentage of .808 is one of the highest for a 20-game winner in league history.

Tiny was at his sharpest in the 1941 World Series' Game 5 when he beat Brooklyn, 3–1, at Ebbets Field and sewed up another World Championship for McCarthy. Tiny went the route, scattering four hits and permitting only two Dodgers to reach base over the last six innings. His command was such that he needed only seven pitches to collect the six outs of innings six and seven.

Tiny had a 5–8 mark in 1946 and was traded to Pittsburgh. He went 24–22 over the next three seasons and died suddenly from complications of an appendicitis attack in a Pittsburgh hospital on September 15, 1949.

All-Star

Ernie Bonham was selected to the American League's All-Star teams in 1942 and 1943, but circumstances conspired to keep him from pitching. In the 1942 game, McCarthy used only two pitchers and

Tiny wasn't one of them. The next year McCarthy, to prove a point, defeated the National League without using any of his Yankee players.

Yankee Stats

	W	L	PCT	G	GS	CG	SA	SO	ERA
7 Years	79	50	.569	158	141	91	6	348	2.73
3 World Series	1	2	.333	4	3	2	0	14	2.89

All-Star Games (no appearances)

ERNIE BONHAM

HANK BOROWY

Career

A crack brigade of Yankee scouts in the 1930s dug up talent all over the country, but the Yankees didn't have far to go to find Hank Borowy. A baseball player at Bloomfield High School in northern New Jersey and Fordham University in the Bronx, Henry Ludwig Borowy excelled right before their eyes. He won 26 straight games at Fordham, where, so far as the Yankees were concerned, he could finish the season before they would sign him. But when scout Paul Krichell discovered that the Red Sox had made a bid for Hank, he made an offer Hank couldn't refuse. Krichell's pen was out of ink, though, and by the time he returned with a working pen Borowy upped the ante by $500, to $8,500. "After that I never traveled without two pens," Krichell said.

Borowy, 26 when he came up to the Yankees in 1942, won his first six games and went 15–4 in his rookie year with an ERA of 2.52. The right-hander won 14 games on the 1943 World Championship club and beat St. Louis in a key game in the World Series. He was the single jewel on a war-depleted 1944 staff, leading the Yankees with 17 wins and in eight other major pitching categories.

Yankee President Larry MacPhail caused a stir by selling Borowy's contract to the Chicago Cubs in July of 1945—with Hank's record at 10–5. The Yankees got nearly $100,000, but the Cubs got a pitcher who would go 11–2 and win two games for them in the 1945 World Series. Borowy's combined 1945 record of 21–7 makes him one of only three modern pitchers to win 20 games while working in both leagues. He would go on to compile a lifetime record of 108–82, completing his career in the majors in 1951.

All-Star

Hank Borowy started the 1944 All-Star Game, played at Pittsburgh's Forbes Field before a crowd of 29,589, pitched three shutout innings (allowing three hits), and knocked in the American League's only run. He turned over a 1–0 lead, but his successors stumbled and the National League won, 7–1. It was his only appearance in the Summer Classic.

Yankee Stats

	W	L	PCT	G	GS	CG	SA	SO	ERA
4 Years	56	30	.651	107	96	53	3	340	2.75
2 World Series	1	0	1.000	2	2	0	0	5	6.55
All-Star Games	0	0	.000	1	1	0	0	0	0.00

HANK BOROWY

JIM BOUTON

Career

Younger fans may know him more for his literary talents, but for at least two seasons, 1963 and 1964, Jim Bouton was a fine right-hander—one of the best in Yankee history.

Bouton, a native of Newark, was signed as a 19-year-old out of Western Michigan University. After a 13–7 record at Amarillo, he was invited to the Yanks' 1962 spring camp as a nonroster player. He impressed Manager Ralph Houk enough to survive the final spring cuts and make the squad.

Bouton had a great fastball and mound charisma. He quickly became a Stadium favorite. The fans enjoyed Bouton's tendency to lose his cap while pitching, the result of his straight overhand delivery. Off the field, Bouton aroused suspicions by reading the sort of books intellectuals might dip into. Yet teammates admired his competitiveness and tagged him "Bulldog."

Bouton followed a 7–7 rookie season with a great 1963. He hurled six shutouts, allowed only 191 hits in 249 innings, posted a 2.53 ERA, and was 21–7. Only Whitey Ford (24–7) won more games in the American League. Jim's 20th win, a shutout against Minnesota, clinched the pennant for New York.

Bouton began the 1964 season slowly, but won 13 games over the second half and finished at 18–13 to lead the Yanks in wins. He added two more victories in the World Series against St. Louis. He was a workhorse in 1964, leading the league in starts with 37.

Arm troubles plagued Bouton after his two sterling years. His combined 1965–68 record was 9–24. The Yankees sold his contract to the expansion Seattle Pilots in October of 1968. Jim left the majors after the 1970 season but made a much-publicized return in 1978. Armed with a knuckleball, he was 1–3 for Atlanta the second time around, his career mark falling below .500 to 62–63.

All-Star

Jim Bouton was selected to the American League's pitching staff for the 1963 All-Star Game in Cleveland. He pitched a perfect sixth inning in a game won by the Nationals, 5–3.

Yankee Stats

	W	L	PCT	G	GS	CG	SA	SO	ERA
7 Years	55	51	.519	197	131	32	4	561	3.36
2 World Series	2	1	.667	3	3	1	0	11	1.48
All-Star Games	0	0	.000	1	0	0	0	0	0.00

JIM BOUTON (NY Yankees)

TOMMY BYRNE

Career

Tommy Byrne, a Baltimorean who starred at Wake Forest University, signed with the Yankees in 1940 reportedly for an unprecedented $10,000. However, it was not until eight years later, what with minor league seasoning and an intervening World War II, that Byrne became a permanent part of the Yankee pitching staff.

The hard-throwing left-hander had fine back-to-back seasons in 1949 (15–7) and 1950 (15–9), and over one stretch that included parts of both seasons won 17 of 19 decisions. But Yankee co-owner Dan Topping had Byrne traded to St. Louis early in the 1951 season. The reason: Topping, who rarely involved himself in personnel matters, was getting a case of frayed nerves watching Byrne pitch. Byrne was the slowest worker in the league.

His games were endless. Besides having a natural inclination to work deliberately, the talented Byrne had control problems that made for baserunners and extended contests. He led the league in hit batsmen in five straight years (1948–52) and in walks three years in a row (1949–51). He once walked 16 men while pitching for the Browns in an extra-inning game.

Byrne bounced around the American League, picked up a load of pitching know-how one winter while playing in Venezuela, and had a successful season with Seattle of the Pacific Coast League. The Yankees bought his contract late in the 1954 season. Tommy had developed a couple of breaking pitches, and although he wasn't as fast as before, he was a more complete pitcher in his second tour with New York.

Byrne won Comeback Player of the Year honors in 1955. He had a record of 16–5 and a league-leading winning percentage of .762. Along the way, he pitched two three-hitters and five four-hitters, and in the World Series five-hit Brooklyn, becoming the season's first southpaw to complete a game against the Dodgers.

Byrne was a good power hitter and was often employed as a pinch-hitter by Casey Stengel, who didn't appreciate the 1951 deal that took Tommy away. In 601 major league at bats, Tommy tagged 14 home runs and drove in 98 runs. He hit better than .300 in two seasons.

The 1957 season was Byrne's 13th and last in the majors. He had only two losing seasons in 11 Yankee campaigns. His .643 winning percentage ranks in the top 10 among all former Yankee pitchers with at least 100 decisions.

All-Star
Tommy Byrne was a member of the American League team for the 1950 All-Star Game played at Comiskey Park. The Americans dropped a 4–3 decision in 14 innings and used six pitchers, but Byrne wasn't called on.

Yankee Stats

	W	L	PCT	G	GS	CG	SA	SO	ERA
11 Years	72	40	.643	221	118	42	12	592	3.93
4 World Series	1	1	.500	6	3	1	0	11	2.53
All-Star Games (no appearances)									

TOMMY BYRNE (NY Yankees)

CHRIS CHAMBLISS

Career

Chris Chambliss' towering home run against Kansas City in the bottom of the ninth gave the Yankees a 7–6 win and their first pennant in 12 years. The date, October 14, 1976, will long be remembered in Yankeeland. Without question, Chambliss' playoff-ending home run was one of baseball history's most dramatic moments, and it was authored by one of baseball's least dramatic performers. If Chambliss, one of the game's genuine clutch hitters, has a hallmark, it is quiet, accomplished consistency, not theatrics.

Chris was born in Dayton, Ohio, but moved often as a youngster as the son of a Navy chaplain. He enjoyed a fine baseball career at UCLA, and with Cleveland in 1971 was named the American League's Rookie of the Year.

The Yankees obtained Chambliss along with Dick Tidrow and Cecil Upshaw in a controversial 1974 deal with the Indians in which New York surrendered four pitchers. Chambliss hit only .243 in 400 Yankee at bats in 1974 and seemed ill at ease in New York. His acquisition cost several popular players and the pressure on him was enormous.

Chris settled down in 1975 and hit his Yankee career high, .304. The next season he drove in 96 runs, his top RBI mark as a Yankee, and in 1979 hit 18 homers. Chris has a classic and fluid left-handed swing that produces line drives to all fields, and he rarely slumps. He averaged 92 RBIs per season over New York's pennant-winning seasons of 1976–78. He hit .524 (and set many batting records) in the 1976 Championship Series and .313 in the World Series that followed.

Chambliss is durable and reliable at first base. For each of five seasons, from 1975 through 1979, he played in at least 149 games. The soft-spoken Chambliss quietly did his job day after day. He made himself into one of the best first basemen in the business and excelled at saving poor throws. He led the league's first sackers in fielding (.997) in 1978 and won a Gold Glove.

The Yankees traded Chambliss to Toronto in November of 1979 as part of the deal that brought Rick Cerone to New York. Chambliss is still playing outstanding baseball for the Atlanta Braves.

All-Star

Chris Chambliss was one of six Yankees selected to the 1976 All-Star Game, which the American League lost, 7–1, in Philadelphia. Chris grounded out as a pinch hitter for Carlton Fisk in the ninth inning.

Yankee Stats

	G	AB	R	H	2B	3B	HR	RBI	BA
6 Years	884	3,382	415	954	171	25	79	454	.282
3 Champ. Series	14	53	6	18	1	1	2	10	.340
3 World Series	13	51	6	14	3	0	1	5	.275
All-Star Games	1	1	0	0	0	0	0	0	.000

CHRIS CHAMBLISS (NY Yankees)

SPUD CHANDLER

Career

Spud Chandler came into the American League with arm troubles, left with arm troubles, and in between—all of it with the Yankees—won 109 games and lost only 43. His .717 winning percentage remains the highest in major league history for former pitchers with at least 100 lifetime decisions.

Spurgeon Ferdinand Chandler, born September 12, 1907, in Commerce, Georgia, was a three-sport star at the University of Georgia. The Yankees signed him after his graduation, and the big right-hander began a long apprenticeship in the minors.

Nearing 30 years of age, Chandler finally made the Yankees in 1937, but arm and shoulder ailments had him shuffling between New York, Newark, and the doctor's office. He posted a fine 14–5 record with the Yankees in 1938 and led the league in fielding at his position. But the following year a broken leg limited his activity to just 11 relief appearances.

Spud developed a slider and in the early 1940s became a complete pitcher. There was no question about his desire, and, indeed, he was one of the fiercest competitors in baseball. He challenged hitters. But he could be a cerebral pitcher, too, "setting up" hitters such as Ted Williams, against whom Chandler had good success. He had the heart and the mind; all he needed were the pitches and a healthy arm.

He had his greatest season in 1943 when he earned league MVP honors. He paced the league in wins (20, against four losses), winning percentage (.833), complete games (20), shutouts (5) and ERA (1.64). He broke Russ Ford's 1910 Yankee ERA record by one percentage point to establish a record that still stands. (Ron Guidry came within 10 points of it in 1978.) Chandler decorated his fine year with two great performances in the 1943 World Series, beating the Cardinals in the opening and final games, 4–2 and 2–0, bringing sweet success to Manager Joe McCarthy in his last World Series.

Having served in the military during World War II, Chandler returned to baseball in 1945. In 1946, his first full postwar season, he went 20–8 with an ERA of 2.10. His 20th win came on the season's final day when he shut out Philadelphia on five hits. He pitched 26 lifetime shutouts, fifth best in Yankee history.

Chandler was still an excellent pitcher in the first half of 1947, pitching 13 consecutive complete games. But bone chips in his right elbow messed up the second half, although he finished 9–5 with a league-leading 2.46 ERA. He made his final appearance in the majors at the age of 40 in the 1947 World Series, courageously working two innings in relief and being touched for two runs.

One week following the World Series, Chandler had seven scraps of cartilage and bone chips removed from his pitching elbow. He retired from baseball the following spring, closing out a tremendous 11-season Yankee career. He never had a losing season.

All-Star

Spud Chandler was a member of the American League's All-Star teams of 1942, 1943, 1946, and 1947. He started the 1942 game, played at the Polo Grounds. He pitched four innings, allowed two hits and no runs, and got credit for the 3–1 American League victory. Spud holds the record for most putouts (three) in an All-Star Game by a pitcher, all three made in the 1942 game. He was not a participant in the other games.

Yankee Stats

	W	L	PCT	G	GS	CG	SA	SO	ERA
11 Years	109	43	.717	211	184	109	6	614	2.84
4 World Series	2	2	.500	6	4	2	1	16	1.62
All-Star Games	1	0	1.000	1	1	0	0	2	0.00

SPUD CHANDLER

BEN CHAPMAN

Career

The Yankees have been considered longballers ever since Mr. Ruth revolutionized the game and set the course for Gehrig, DiMaggio, Mantle, and some other fence-busters. Still, the club has had its base thieves, and none more exciting, daring, or brilliant than Ben Chapman.

Chapman, sometimes called a second Ty Cobb, led the American League in stolen bases three straight years—1931 (61), 1932 (38), and 1933 (27). His 61 thefts in 1931 were the most in the league since Washington's Sam Rice stole 63 in 1920, the year Babe changed the game, and no Yankee has matched it since. Chapman is tied for third on New York's all-time stolen base list with 184 (although Willie Randolph began 1983 with 178). Ben was fast, ran with abandon regardless of the score, and delighted a generation of fans raised on the long ball. He stole home in the majors 14 times.

But Chapman was a complete offensive player. He hit .305 as a Yankee, making him one of only seven .300 hitters who played at least 500 games with the Yankees. He hit .315 in 1931 with 17 homers and 122 RBIs. He belted three home runs in a 1932 game, two of them inside-the-parkers! He also had a three-triples game (as an Indian) in 1939.

The native of Nashville, Tennessee, was a 21-year-old Yankee rookie in 1930, coming off a year in St. Paul in which he hit .336 with 31 homers and 137 RBIs. He hit .316, playing 91 games at third base and 45 at second. He had a strong arm but he wasn't always accurate, especially on short throws; in 1931, Joe McCarthy, the Yanks' new manager, moved Ben to left field where his speed and strong arm were used to better advantage. Twice Ben led league outfielders in assists. He became so good that in 1934 he was shifted to center field.

Chapman's one weakness—in McCarthy's eyes, at least—was his temper. He was incendiary, or perhaps more accurately and fairly, fiery. McCarthy, however, preferred his professionals on the cool side. So Chapman, who had kept center field warm until a rookie named Joe DiMaggio was ready to handle the job, was traded to Washington in June of 1936. His career continued to flourish and he went on to play a total of 15 years in the majors with an average of .302.

All-Star
Ben Chapman was an All-Star for the first three years of the Summer Classic, 1933–35. Leading off the bottom of the first inning in the 1933 game, he became the first American League batter in All-Star Game history. He played left and right field and had one hit in five trips, as the Americans won, 4–2, at Comiskey Park. The next year he substituted for Ruth in right field, made an assist, and tripled in two trips. In the 1935 game he was a defensive replacement in left field.

Yankee Stats

	G	AB	R	H	2B	3B	HR	RBI	BA
7 Years	909	3,539	626	1,079	209	54	60	589	.305
1 World Series	4	17	1	5	2	0	0	6	.294
All-Star Games	3	7	0	2	0	1	0	0	.286

BEN CHAPMAN

JIM COATES

Career

Any pitcher who in four seasons with one club racks up a .712 winning percentage has achieved something special. Jim Coates did just that, going 37–15 over the 1959–62 seasons. Jim served the Yankees in those years as a spot starter and long reliever, making the right-hander's accomplishment all the more impressive.

The lanky country boy from Farnham, Virginia, played hardball in the figurative as well as literal sense. He would brush a pushy hitter off the plate without a second thought. Coates entered the Yankee farm system in 1952, armed with a great fastball that was not easily harnessed. He had a cup of coffee in 1956 and made the Yankees in 1959.

Over the 1959–60 seasons, Coates had a 13-game win streak that included his first nine decisions of 1960 and reached 13 on June 29, 1960, when he three-hit Kansas City and won, 10–0. He had good support; in his 14 starts during the streak, New York averaged 8.4 runs per game.

Coates was 13–3 in 1960, 11–5 in 1961, and 7–6 with six saves in 1962. He came through in the clutch when Whitey Ford was injured in Game 4 of the 1961 World Series, pitching the final four innings and combining with Ford to blank Cincinnati. He was dealt to Washington in April of 1963.

All-Star

Jim Coates was on the American League's roster for both All-Star Games in 1960. He appeared in only the first game, in Kansas City, pitching two-hit shutout ball over the fourth and fifth innings. The Nationals won, 5–3.

Yankee Stats

	W	L	PCT	G	GS	CG	SA	SO	ERA
5 Years	37	15	.712	167	39	12	15	284	3.84
3 World Series	0	1	.000	6	0	0	1	8	4.15
All-Star Games	0	0	.000	1	0	0	0	0	0.00

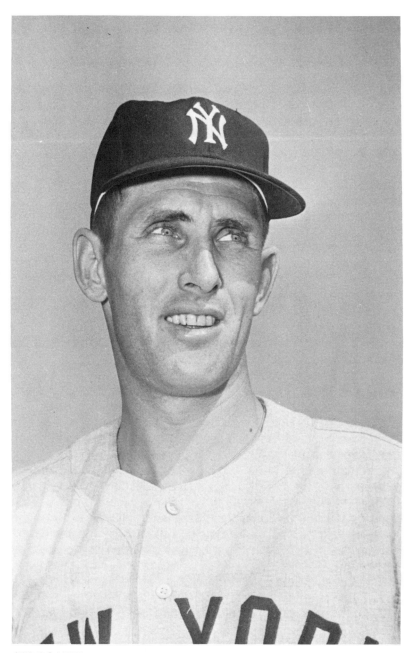

JIM COATES (NY Yankees)

JERRY COLEMAN

Career

Duty twice called Jerry Coleman from his chosen field, once in World War II and again in the Korean War. The second call interrupted one of the finest careers in baseball, and Jerry Coleman never really regained the outstanding form he showed before his second military tour.

Coleman, who was born in 1924 in San Jose, California, signed with the Yankees in 1942 after his graduation from high school. He spent one season in the minors and three years in the service, flying 57 fighter missions in the Pacific. Coleman returned to the Yankee organization in 1946, and in three minor league seasons earned a reputation as an exceptionally adroit and acrobatic infielder.

In the spring camp of 1949, Casey Stengel moved Coleman from shortstop to second base where Jerry continued his fancy fielding. If anything, he was even more magnificent at second, fielding .981 in his rookie year to lead the league at his position. He hit a solid .275 and came through in the season's final game; thanks largely to Coleman's three-run hit, the Yankees, locked with Boston, beat the Red Sox, 5–3, to capture the pennant.

Coleman was even better in 1950, hitting .287 with 69 RBIs and winning the Babe Ruth Award as the top player in the World Series. He participated in 137 double plays. Coupled with shortstop Phil Rizzuto's 123, the keystone combo totaled 260 double plays, one of the highest totals in American League history. Rizzuto and Coleman may have been the best double-play team in Yankee history.

Coleman was the Yanks' regular second baseman in 1951 for the third year in a row. But the following May, with his average a gaudy .405 (17-for-42), Jerry returned to military service. He rejoined the Yankees late in the 1953 season as a utility infielder, although the following year he had 300 at bats. He spent three months on the disabled list in 1955 after breaking his collarbone in a collision at home plate.

The Korean call-up put a crimp in Coleman's baseball career. As a regular before entering the service, Jerry hit .277 (380-for-1,373) in 413 games. As a part-timer after his return, he hit .239 (178-for-746) in 310 games.

He hit .364 in the 1957 World Series and then hung up his spikes. A gentleman and a class guy, Coleman moved into the Yankee front office and a few years later was broadcasting Yankee games with Rizzuto and company.

All-Star
Jerry Coleman was an All-Star in 1950. He replaced starter Bobby Doerr at second base and went hitless in two at bats in a game the Nationals won, 4–3, in 14 innings at Comiskey Park.

Yankee Stats

	G	AB	R	H	2B	3B	HR	RBI	BA
9 Years	723	2,119	267	558	77	18	16	217	.263
6 World Series	26	69	6	19	6	0	0	9	.275
All-Star Games	1	2	0	0	0	0	0	0	.000

JERRY COLEMAN (NY Yankees)

FRANK CROSETTI

Career

Frank Crosetti wore the pinstripes from 1932 through 1968 and was a member of more pennant-winning clubs than anyone in history—23, as a player and coach. He was an always-in-shape athlete who approached the game with a quiet but tough dedication. He was a winner and a real professional.

Crosetti, who was born in San Francisco, made an immediate impact on Yankee fortunes in 1932 as a 22-year-old rookie. He was the only change among the eight regulars on a team that won 94 games in 1931 and finished a distant second. But the 1932 Yanks, with Crosetti at shortstop for 83 games and at third base for 33 more, won 107 games and a runaway pennant. The Crow, who was acquired from the San Francisco Seals, held together the infield's left side, previously the Achilles' heel of the Yankee defense.

Crosetti was the Yankee shortstop through 1940. When Phil Rizzuto, the spectacular rookie who took over the job in 1941, entered the navy, Frank was back at short (1943–45, although he held a job in a defense plant for the first half of the 1944 season). Rizzuto returned in 1946 and the Crow became his backup.

As an infielder, Crosetti had a great arm, but he was more dependable than spectacular. He led league shortstops in three major fielding categories in both the 1938 and 1939 seasons. He also played a neat third base and appeared in 131 games there, 62 of them in 1942.

His best hitting year was 1936 when he batted .288 and collected 15 homers and 78 RBIs. He had great hand strength and his 14 game-opening homers places him among baseball's all-time leaders in leading off a game with a home run. He scored 137 runs in 1936 and topped the 100-runs-scored mark in each of the 1936–39 championship seasons. He also ran well and led the league in stolen bases in 1938 with 27.

Statistics provide an unfinished portrait of Crosetti as the sparkplug and doer of whatever it took to win. An expert at drawing walks (he is sixth on New York's all-time list with 792), Frank hoped to also reach base by getting his oversized uniform top nicked by close pitches. He led the league eight times in being hit by pitched balls. He was a skilled practitioner of the "hidden ball trick" and a tremendous stealer of signs. If there was an edge to be gained, the Crow would gain it.

The Yankees in 1947 signed Crosetti as a player-coach. He became a fulltime coach in 1949 and for 20 seasons served as the Yankees' third base coach and infield instructor. Taciturn though he was, he helped develop many players and, in spite of a stern demeanor, the Crow took several players under his wing.

All-Star

Frank Crosetti was a member of the American League's 1936 and 1939 All-Star teams. In the 1936 game, he struck out as a pinch-hitter in the ninth inning of a 4–3 National League win at Braves Field in Boston. Frank didn't get to play in the 1939 game at Yankee Stadium.

Yankee Stats

	G	AB	R	H	2B	3B	HR	RBI	BA
17 Years	1,682	6,277	1,006	1,541	260	65	98	649	.245
7 World Series	29	115	16	20	5	1	1	11	.174
All-Star Games	1	1	0	0	0	0	0	0	.000

FRANK CROSETTI (NY Yankees)

Career

Pitcher Ron Davis redefined the role of the long reliever and gave respectability to one of baseball's least appreciated jobs.

Davis, a long, lean right-hander from Houston who was obtained in a 1978 trade with the Cubs (and dealt to Minnesota in the 1982 Roy Smalley acquisition), was the beneficiary of a brilliant conversion. Headed nowhere as a starter in the Cubs' lower minors, Ron was turned into a relief pitcher by the Yankees. He made a quick and successful transition, going 9–2 at West Haven and making four appearances in New York (without a decision) late in 1978.

When an injury to Gossage made a shambles of New York's bullpen in May of 1979, Davis was called up from Columbus. He worked in 44 games in 1979 and broke the American League rookie record for relief wins, a record set by the Yanks' Wilcy Moore in 1927, with a 14–2 record.

The Gossage-Davis bullpen tandem in the 1980–81 seasons was the closest thing to perfection the American League has ever seen; the Yankees went 130–5 for games in which they took a lead into the seventh inning. Davis would often work the sixth, seventh, or eighth innings, before handing the ball to Gossage. The Yankees were revolutionizing baseball, but seldom did Ron get statistical credit. (In a system devised by the Elias Sports Bureau, and published in *Sports Illustrated*, Davis in 1981 led the league in "holds" with 21.)

But Davis did gain a measure of fame in 1981 by striking out 83 batters in 73 innings. On May 4, 1981, he fanned eight Angels in a row to set a major league record for relievers. Ron, who had developed a rising fastball (to go with his sinking fastball), struck out 14 of 15 batters over three games!

All-Star

Ron Davis was added to the American League's All-Star roster in 1981 as a replacement for an injured Gossage. He allowed one run in one inning of work and struck out one.

Yankee Stats

	W	L	PCT	G	GS	CG	SA	SO	ERA
4 Years	27	10	.730	144	0	0	22	191	2.94
2 Champ. Series	0	0	.000	3	0	0	0	7	1.23
1 World Series	0	0	.000	4	0	0	0	4	23.14
All-Star Games	0	0	.000	1	0	0	0	1	9.00

RON DAVIS (NY Yankees)

BUCKY DENT

Career

New York trailed Boston, 2–0, in a one-game playoff for the 1978 championship of the American League's East Division when a three-run Bucky Dent homer gave the Yanks a lead they would not relinquish. For that, the handsome Mr. Dent will forever be remembered, or at least for as long as Boston and New York compete in baseball.

The Yankees obtained Dent, born in Savannah, Georgia, and raised in Florida, in a deal with the White Sox just before Opening Day in 1977. Only 25, Dent already was a four-year veteran of the bigs. Russell Earl Dent hit .247 in his first Yankee season and put glue in the infield (the Yankees would have the league's best infield in the late 1970s). And New York won its first World Championship in 15 years.

Dent isn't spectacular defensively, but he doesn't have to be—he positions himself better than any shortstop in baseball. And when a clutch play is needed in the ninth inning of a close game, he is not likely to flub it. He teamed with Willie Randolph to form one of the best double-play combinations in Yankee history. Dent led league shortstops in 1980 with a .982 fielding percentage, only one point off the Yankee record.

The 1978 season, injury-plagued and discouraging for Dent, tested Bucky's mettle; he came through with clutch hits down the stretch. Capping everything, he hit .417 against the Dodgers in the World Series and was named the Series' MVP. He became a national celebrity. He was on posters and in parades, and he made television and movie appearances, his boyish good looks not hurting.

Dent tore ligaments in his hand in August of 1981 and was lost for the year. Just before Opening Day in 1982, the Yankees obtained shortstop Roy Smalley, who shared shortstop with Bucky. But Bucky hated being platooned and played poorly. Early in August of 1982, with his average at .169 in 59 games, Bucky was dealt to Texas. "One of the most outstanding young men we've ever had," said George Steinbrenner of the departing Dent. Capable, hard-working, tough, decent, and clutch—Bucky was indeed outstanding.

All-Star

Bucky Dent was selected as the American League's starting shortstop in both the 1980 and 1981 All-Star Games. He went 1-for-2 in the 1980 game and 2-for-2 (single and double) in the 1981 game. Bucky's

.750 average is the highest among Yankees who have played in at least two All-Star Games. Despite his poor 1982, the fans still recognized him as a premier performer—he finished second to Robin Yount in the All-Star balloting.

Yankee Stats

	G	AB	R	H	2B	3B	HR	RBI	BA
6 Years	695	2,163	229	518	81	10	27	209	.239
3 Champ. Series	6	12	40	1	8	1	0	0	.200
2 World Series	12	43	3	15	1	0	0	9	.349
All-Star Games	2	4	0	3	1	0	0	0	.750

BUCKY DENT (NY Yankees)

BILL DICKEY

Career

Bill Dickey was inducted into the Baseball Hall of Fame in 1954 and in 1969 was voted the game's Greatest Living Catcher. He and Yogi Berra have had their jointly held Yankee uniform number (8) retired by the club. By all measures he is among the Yankee (and the game's) immortals, but how Bill Dickey got to be a Yankee was something of an "accident."

Born June 6, 1907, in Bastrop, Louisiana, Dickey spent most of his youth around Little Rock, Arkansas, where indeed he has spent much of his life. An infielder and pitcher in high school, he began to catch at Little Rock College. Next came a four-year minor league career, including several stints with the Little Rock club that at the time had a working agreement with the Chicago White Sox. Most major league executives assumed that Bill was obligated to Chicago, but Johnny Nee, who scouted Dickey for the Yankees, discovered he was under contract only to Little Rock. Based on Nee's ringing endorsement, the Yankees bought Dickey's contract and never regretted it. Bill's 17 exceptional seasons were exclusively on behalf of New York.

Dickey joined the Yankees late in the 1928 season and played in 10 games. In 1929 he assumed the first-string catching job and for 13 straight years caught at least 100 games, a league record. He played only at catcher and ranks sixth in history with 1,712 games caught. No one ahead of him on that list owns a .300 lifetime average, however. Dickey hit .313, a remarkable career average for a catcher.

In 1936, Dickey hit .362, the highest average in history for a catcher playing in at least 100 games behind the plate. The following season he had 133 RBIs, another league record for a catcher. Also in 1937, Dickey hit 29 home runs, the league record for catchers until Yogi Berra's 30 in 1952. He is the only major league catcher ever to register 20 homers and 100 RBIs over four consecutive seasons, and in those seasons, 1936–39, New York won four straight World Championships.

Dickey was a consistently powerful left-handed swinger. (Berra is the only American League catcher to have outhomered Dickey lifetime.) Dickey wasn't a lumbering slugger, either. He had more home runs than strikeouts in five seasons. It is hard to find a better hitting catcher in history than Bill Dickey, who in 1943, at the age of 36, hit .351 in 85 games. He hit in the clutch, too. In the 1932 World

Series sweep of the Cubs, Dickey batted .438 in his first Fall Classic. In 1943, in his final World Series game as a player, he walloped a two-run homer; the Yankees beat St. Louis, 2–0, to win another World Championship, one of eight championships Dickey enjoyed as a Yankee player.

As great a hitter as Dickey was, catching may have been the best part of his game. Detroit's Charlie Gehringer said Dickey "made catching look easy." In 1931, Bill played in 125 games behind the plate and did not make a single passed ball. Four times he led the league's catchers in fielding average. At 6'1", he was considered tall for a catcher in his day, but Bill was agile and had enormous range around the plate. He was great at catching foul pops. He had a strong and

BILL DICKEY (NY Yankees)

deadly-accurate throwing arm. He was baseball-smart and a clear-thinking field general. He was a fine shaper of young pitchers, and no pitcher, young or old, was inclined to shake him off, so thorough was his control of the game.

Experts differ as to whether Dickey or his rival of several years, Mickey Cochrane, is baseball's greatest catcher. Black Mike was great and hit .320 lifetime, but Dickey hit for much more power, and most contemporaries report that Dickey had the stronger arm. Both were leaders in their own ways. Dickey led quietly. He played the 1936 World Series with a hand fractured in two places, keeping news of the injury to himself.

Dickey was in the navy during the 1944–45 seasons and returned to the Yankees as backup catcher in 1946. When Joe McCarthy resigned in May, Bill found himself managing the Yankees, a job he himself resigned in September. But he wasn't gone for long, returning for many seasons as one of Casey Stengel's able coaches.

For over 50 years, Bill Dickey has been one of the grand gentlemen of the National Pastime, and a gentleman is what he has always been. A few years ago Bill said on receiving the Pride of the Yankees Award, "I am often asked what I think of today's high salaries and if I would have liked to have played now. That, naturally, made me think for a moment. As I thought of the men I played with and the pennants we won, I knew I had played in the best of times and wouldn't change it for anything."

All-Star

Starting in the first All-Star Game in 1933, Bill Dickey was selected to the American League's team 11 times. He was in the service in 1944–45; otherwise, he was an All-Star in every year that he was eligible except 1935. He played in eight games. His most memorable was the 1934 game at the Polo Grounds when Carl Hubbell struck out Babe Ruth, Lou Gehrig, Jimmie Foxx, Al Simmons, and Joe Cronin in succession, before Dickey halted the streak with a single. Bill's best game was in 1937, when the Americans won, 8–3, in Washington, Bill collecting a single and double while scoring once and knocking in a run.

Yankee Stats

	G	AB	R	H	2B	3B	HR	RBI	BA
17 Years	1,789	6,300	930	1,969	343	72	202	1,209	.313
8 World Series	38	145	19	37	1	1	5	24	.255
All-Star Games	8	19	3	5	2	0	0	1	.263

JOE DiMAGGIO

Career

Joe DiMaggio excelled physically and mentally and was probably the greatest all-round player in baseball history. He excelled in every aspect of the game—hitting for average and power, running, throwing, and fielding. And he was alert. He never missed a sign in his entire career. On the bases, he knew when to try for an extra base, and in center field, he never threw to a wrong base. Joe DiMaggio studied the game although his studiousness, overwhelmed by his tremendous natural talent, tended to be overlooked. He was a hardworking, inspiring ballplayer over whose 13 seasons the Yankees won 10 pennants and nine World Series. Yeah, but could DiMaggio bunt? "I don't know," his skipper, Joe McCarthy, replied. "Nor have I any intention of ever finding out."

A son of Italian immigrants, Joe was born in Martinez, California, on November 25, 1914. He grew up in San Francisco, where he broke into professional baseball in 1932 with the Seals. In only his second year in baseball he hit .340 and had a stunning 61-game hitting streak. By the spring of 1934, Joe DiMaggio was considered the minors' best prospect. But as he was climbing hurriedly out of a taxi, his knee "popped like a pistol," and the pop was heard around the major leagues. Most scouts backed off, but not Yankee scouts Bill Essick and Joe Devine, who, along with Farm Director George Weiss, urged Yankee Owner Jacob Ruppert to obtain the young DiMaggio. The deal was made in November of 1934. San Francisco got five players, $25,000 or more, and the right to keep Joe one more year—1935, when he hit .398 and was the Pacific Coast League's MVP.

DiMaggio's Yankee career was interrupted by a three-year hitch (three prime years) in the military during World War II. In the years 1936–42, he was the supreme figure in baseball, piling up great stats on great teams. In the years 1946–51, he was beset by injuries and encroaching age, and his overall stats were less impressive, yet his stature grew. These postwar Yankee teams were not as strong as those of Joe's earlier years, and when Boston raced to an easy pennant in 1946, as baseball returned to normalcy, some experts saw the dawn of a Beantown dynasty. But DiMaggio would have none of that; he led the Yankees to World Championships in 1947, 1949, 1950, and 1951.

Joe began his Yankee career in 1936 with a bang. He hit .323 on the season and .346 in the World Series and set rookie records for runs scored (132) and triples (15). In his sophomore year, he won the home-run title with 46, most ever by a Yankee right-handed batter, and in 1939 he won the first of two consecutive batting titles with a .381 average. He was also the league's MVP that year, an honor he reclaimed in 1941, the year of his famous 56-game hitting streak. He won his third MVP in 1947 and his second home-run and RBI titles in 1948—his best postwar season—with 39 and 155 respectively. (No Yankee has since approached 155 RBIs.) In 1949, after becoming baseball's first $100,000 a year ballplayer, he missed the first 65 games because of an injury and then made a miraculous comeback.

Swinging from his classic right-handed stance, with feet wide apart, Joe waited until the last instant before whipping his bat in a level swing made powerful by exceptionally strong wrists. In his first seven seasons, he averaged 133 RBIs per season; one year, 1937, he had an RBI total (167) that was 16 more than his games-played total (151). For a power hitter he had incredible bat control, hitting 361 homers and striking out only 369 times. Reggie Jackson, to take another slugger, homered 409 times and struck out 1,682 times in his first 13 seasons (1968–80).

DiMaggio averaged 28 homers for his 13 Yankee seasons, an amazing total for a righty at Yankee Stadium, especially since Death Valley in Joe's day was far more spacious than it is today. The right-handed hitter who ranks immediately behind DiMaggio's 361 Yankee home runs is Tony Lazzeri; he hit 169—not half the Yankee Clipper's total. Joe won two home-run crowns; Bob Meusel is the only other right-handed Yankee to win the homer title, and he won one. Joe played in a ballpark that was not to his advantage, but as he once said, "I'm getting paid to hit the long ball and I hit best by pulling to left. If I changed my swing and tried to punch it to right, I might lose my rhythm and not be able to hit anywhere." He hit eight World Series home runs and is tied with Bill Skowron and Frank Robinson for the most by a righty.

Defensively, center fielder DiMaggio was the greatest. He got a tremendous jump and his first step was always the correct one. He didn't showboat or make diving catches. He was usually there in plenty of time to make a "routine" catch. In each of four seasons, DiMaggio led the league's outfielders in assists, putouts, double plays, and fielding average.

DiMaggio had two storybook seasons. In 1941, he hit safely in 56 straight games. The streak began on May 15, at a time when New

JOE DiMAGGIO (NY Yankees)

York was losing consistently, and ended on July 17, with the Yankees steamrolling toward an easy pennant. Joe hit .408 over the 56 games. The game after that streak ended, he started a 16-game hitting streak. Not surprising. He had, before the great streak that captivated the nation, three streaks of better than 20 games.

DiMaggio made his 1949 season debut in a big June series in Boston after being sidelined with a heel injury. In a three-game Yankee sweep, Joe hit four homers, drove in nine runs, and ended all question of his supremacy. He finished the year at .346 with 14 homers and 67 RBIs in only 272 at bats. But he was hospitalized in September with pneumonia. He did play the final two games of the season and the Yankees won both, from Boston, to win the pennant. On Joe DiMaggio Day, he summed up by saying, "And I want to thank the Good Lord for making me a Yankee."

On December 11, 1951, DiMaggio, after a .263 year, retired rather than play below his personal standards. More than three decades later, he remains the greatest name in baseball. His No. 5 uniform was retired by the Yankees and in 1955 he was inducted into the Baseball Hall of Fame. In a nationwide poll conducted in 1969, DiMaggio was voted baseball's Greatest Living Player.

All-Star

Joe DiMaggio was picked to the American League's All-Star team in all 13 seasons of his career and he played in 11 of the games (he was injured one year). In the 1939 game, he delighted 62,892 at Yankee Stadium by walloping a homer off the Cubs' Bill Lee in a 3–1 American League victory. Joe came into the 1941 game with his hitting streak at 48 games, doubled off the Cubs' Claude Passeau, and scored three runs in a 7–5 win by the Americans. He had three RBIs, two hits, and one run scored in the 1949 game played in Brooklyn and won by the Americans, 11–7.

Yankee Stats

	G	AB	R	H	2B	3B	HR	RBI	BA
13 Years	1,736	6,821	1,390	2,214	389	131	361	1,537	.325
10 World Series	51	199	27	54	6	0	8	30	.271
All-Star Games	11	40	7	9	2	0	1	6	.225

Career

Al Downing fanned 10 or more batters 17 times in his major league career, a statistic that puts him in the legendary company of Warren Spahn, Bobo Newsom, and Denny McLain. One of the hardest throwers in Yankee history, his fastball was "live" and he was, indeed, a strikeout artist, ranking seventh on the club's all-time strikeout list with 1,028. But he was more than a strikeout specialist; he was an excellent pitcher. His 3.25 ERA as a Yankee is among the top 20 in the club's history.

Scout Bill Yancey signed Downing out of Trenton, New Jersey, for the Yankees. Al, at Binghamton in 1961, his first professional season, went 9–1 with a 1.84 ERA and learned much from Manager Jimmy Gleeson. Downing appeared in six games for New York over the 1961–62 campaigns and spun a no-hitter at Richmond, where he pitched in 1962.

The Yankees brought Downing up from Richmond for keeps in June of 1963. He made his first start in Washington on June 11 and pitched a two-hit, nine-strikeout shutout; at the Stadium July 2 he blanked Chicago on one hit. He maintained this electric pace all summer and at 22 became an instant sensation and the first black pitcher in the Yanks' regular starting rotation. Downing finished the year, 13–5. He struck out 171 in 176 innings and had a 2.56 ERA. He allowed only 5.84 hits per nine innings for one of the best single-season ratios in baseball history.

Al went 13–8 in 1964 and had a league-leading 217 strikeouts, breaking Whitey Ford's club record of 209 southpaw strikeouts. Ron Guidry's 248 strikeouts in 1978 broke Downing's record, but Downing remains third on the club's single-season list (for both righties and lefties) behind Guidry and Jack Chesbro. The right-handed Chesbro fanned 239 in 1904.

Downing pitched 200 or more innings in each season from 1964 to 1967 and always led the Yankees in strikeouts. He was better than his teams. His 1967 record of 14–10, for example, computes to a winning percentage of .583 while the 1967 Yankees played only .444 ball. His 2.63 ERA suggests he may have been a 20-game winner on a better club, especially since he was a complete pitcher, having mastered a change-of-pace pitch. But he still had the old smoke, too. On May 24, 1967, he two-hit Baltimore, striking out 13 Orioles.

When it seemed Downing was reaching the upper echelons of the pitching profession, he developed a sore arm and in 1968 went 3–3. He was 7–5 the following year as a fifth starter and long reliever, then in December was traded to Oakland. Two years later Al won 20 games for the Dodgers.

All-Star

Al Downing and Mickey Mantle were the only Yankees selected for the American League team for the 1967 All-Star Game in Anaheim, California. Downing pitched the ninth and 10th innings, blanked the Nationals, and kept the game tied at 1–1, in the process fanning two great hitters—Roberto Clemente and Richie Allen. Downing turned over the tie game, which the Nationals won, 2–1, in 15 innings, to young Catfish Hunter.

Yankee Stats

	W	L	PCT	G	GS	CG	SA	SO	ERA
9 Years	72	57	.558	208	175	46	2	1,028	3.25
2 World Series	0	2	.000	4	2	0	0	11	7.10
All-Star Games	0	0	.000	1	0	0	0	2	0.00

AL DOWNING (NY Yankees)

RYNE DUREN

Career

"I would not admire hitting against Duren because if he ever hit you in the head you might be in the past tense," Casey Stengel once said in speaking of his relief ace, Rinold George Duren. No doubt about it, Ryne Duren was the most intimidating pitcher of his time. His fastball was officially clocked in 1960 at 91.1 mph (Rich Gossage was clocked at 99.4 mph in 1980), but a few years earlier Duren could get it up near 100. A combination of speed, frequent wildness, and poor eyesight scared the devil out of every sane hitter in the league. The Stadium crowd enjoyed his act as much as it savored Gossage's 20 years later.

Duren, who was born February 22, 1929, in Cazenovia, Wisconsin, broke into pro ball in 1949, walking 114 men in 85 innings at Wausau. Control problems plagued him for years. The Yankees obtained him in a 1957 trade that sent Billy Martin to the Kansas City A's. Duren, finally wearing the proper corrective lens ("coke bottles" in Stengel's vernacular), could see the plate and finished 13–2 at Denver, a Yankee farm club.

Duren was a Yankee star in 1958, leading the league in saves with 20 and winning *The Sporting News*' Rookie Pitcher of the Year award. He was a star in the World Series, saving Game 3 and winning Game 6 with an eight-strikeout, one-run performance over 4 2/3 innings. This was the Series in which the Yankees overcame a three-games-to-one deficit to beat Milwaukee.

The Yankees may have had a poor 1959, but not Duren. For the second consecutive season, he led the club in saves (14) and games pitched (41). His 1.88 ERA, 36-consecutive-scoreless-inning streak, and 96 strikeouts in 77 innings attest to his prowess. He struck out eight of nine batters he faced in a June 26 game with Chicago.

Duren was a holdout in 1960 and came up with a unique way of settling a contract dispute; he decided to accept the average figure of a poll of writers who covered the Yankees. After signing for $17,500, Duren walked 49 men in 49 innings and his ERA ballooned to 4.96. Alcohol abuse was taking its toll on Ryne, however. He courageously conquered his problem (and helped other alcoholics) many years after drifting out of baseball, but at this point Ryne had troubles and in May of 1961 he was dealt to the Angels.

All-Star

Ryne Duren was an All-Star in 1958 and 1959. He didn't pitch in the 1958 game or in the second game of 1959. But in the first 1959 game in Pittsburgh, which the Nationals won, 5–4, Duren blanked the opposition on one hit over the three middle innings, recording four strikeouts along the way.

Yankee Stats

	W	L	PCT	G	GS	CG	SA	SO	ERA
4 Years	12	15	.444	131	2	0	43	257	2.74
2 World Series	1	1	.500	5	0	0	1	19	2.03
All-Star Games	0	0	.000	1	0	0	0	4	0.00

RYNE DUREN (NY Yankees)

WHITEY FORD

Career

In his first 100 big league decisions, Whitey Ford had a .740 winning percentage (74–26), highest through history for 100 decisions. He finished his career at 236–106 for a .690 percentage, highest among twentieth century winners of 200 or more games. Three times he led the American League in wins (1955, 1961, 1963) and winning percentage (1956, 1961, 1963). Fourteen of his 25 wins in 1961 (most wins by a Yankee since Lefty Gomez won 26 in 1934) were won in a row, tying a club record set in 1904 by Jack Chesbro. Eight of those consecutive victories were won in June, making him the first left-hander in league history to win eight games in one month. He owns almost all World Series pitching records, including the most wins (10). Whitey was a winner.

Born in Manhattan on October 21, 1928, Edward Charles Ford grew up in the Astoria section of Queens. He graduated from Manhattan High School of Aviation and played as a first baseman and pitcher in sandlot baseball. Yankee scout Paul Krichell urged Ford to concentrate on pitching. "I never saw a kid with a curveball like his or one who could throw one so easy," the famous scout once said. In October of 1946, Krichell signed Ford to a Yankee contract and a bonus of $7,000.

Ford began his climb through the Yankee farm system with a 13–4 mark at Butler in 1947. Then came seasons of 16–8 at Norfolk and 16–5 at Binghamton. In 1950, Ford was 6–3 at Kansas City, the Yanks' top farm club, when the Yankees sent for him. On July 17, 1950, he beat Chicago for the first of nine consecutive major league wins. (He lost his only decision on September 27 in relief in Philadelphia.) New York finished only three games on top, claiming a pennant it could not have won without Whitey Ford. Whitey won the World Series clincher against the Phillies, then went on to a two-year military hitch at Fort Monmouth, New Jersey. When Ford returned to the Yankees in 1953, he assumed a 14-year reign as the Yankee ace.

At 5'10" and 178 pounds, Ford was not an overpowering pitcher. He was artistic and crafty, keeping hitters off stride with a repertoire of pitches, speeds, and locations, and seldom beating himself. Some called him cute, but he was unremittingly efficient, often using fewer than 100 pitches to dispose of the opposition. He threw a sneaky fastball and a beautiful curve, and both pitches were complemented by a slider he developed in 1961. He was tough to hit; not once in the 14 seasons in which he pitched more than 100 innings did he allow as many hits as the innings he pitched, a remarkable achievement.

Gutty Whitey Ford had nerves of steel and a driving desire to win. He was a great "money pitcher." His boyish looks said one thing, but his body language told another story; he was a lethal weapon on the mound. Yankee pitching coach Jim Turner has said, "I have never seen pressure bother him, and the Yankees during those days were always under pressure." But Whitey was as easy-going off the field as he was down-to-business on it. He had his share of fun in baseball, and if he lost, he didn't fall to despair or point fingers. Teammates, the press, and the fans loved Whitey Ford.

Along with having complete command of his pitches, including some "trick" ones, Ford worked hard on the other aspects of his game. He used a Yankee tour of Japan in 1955 to work on his pick-off move and developed the best move in baseball. Once, having allowed a lead-off triple late in a regular season game in which the Yankees led, 1–0, Ford signaled his third baseman, Andy Carey, and promptly picked off the runner, protecting his slim margin. Ford was also a great fielder and in 1965 led the league's pitchers in fielding average.

In September of 1955 he hurled back-to-back one-hitters, and twice in his career he struck out six consecutive batters. On April 22, 1959, Ford went 14 innings to beat Washington, 1–0, while striking out 15. He pitched 33 2/3 consecutive scoreless innings in World Series competition in the early 1960s, breaking Babe Ruth's record.

Whitey Ford ranks first on the Yanks' all-time list for wins, games pitched, games started, innings pitched, strikeouts, and shutouts. Casey Stengel never started him more than 33 times in one season, generally holding Ford back to pitch against the better clubs and pitchers. But Ralph Houk, who became manager in 1961, worked Whitey every fourth day in a regular rotation. Beginning in 1961, Ford started 39, 37, and 37 games, and won 25, 17, and 24 games. He won the Cy Young Award in 1961.

Ford was bothered by shoulder and arm problems in mid-career and in 1964 developed a circulation problem in his left shoulder. In August of 1966, Whitey underwent surgery to correct a blocked artery in his left shoulder, but in May of 1967, a painful bone spur in Whitey's left elbow worsened and forced his retirement. It was not American League hitters that drove him from the game, not when Whitey was sporting an ERA of 1.64 (over seven starts) at the time of his retirement.

WHITEY FORD

Ford, dubbed the "Chairman of the Board" by Elston Howard, remained connected with the club in several capacities. He pitched 16 Yankee seasons, longer than any other pitcher, and his No. 16 uniform has been retired. In 1974, Ford and pal Mickey Mantle were inducted into the Baseball Hall of Fame together. As Casey Stengel said on the day of their induction, "Yes, sir, they were fairly amazing in several respects, and that's the damn truth!"

All-Star

Whitey Ford was an All-Star in 1954–56, 1958–61, and 1964. He pitched every year in which he was selected except 1958 and 1964, and he set records for most runs (13) and hits (19) allowed. Yet, he pitched well in the three games he started. In the 1954 game, Ford blanked the Nationals on one hit over the first three innings and the Americans went on to an 11–9 victory. In the second game of 1960, played at Yankee Stadium, Whitey permitted three runs over the first three innings and got tagged with the loss. He started the first game of 1961 and pitched well, allowing only one run and two hits over three innings.

Yankee Stats

	W	L	PCT	G	GS	CG	SA	SO	ERA
16 Years	236	106	.690	498	438	156	10	1,956	2.74
11 World Series	10	8	.556	22	22	7	0	94	2.71
All-Star Games	0	2	.000	6	3	0	0	5	5.40

LOU GEHRIG

Career

Lou Gehrig was a big fish in a big, big pond, a pond that included such big fishes as, in overshadowing succession, the great Ruth and the spectacularly gifted DiMaggio, as well as the neighboring Giants' first baseman, Bill Terry, who in 1930 hit .401. Lou was overshadowed but not eclipsed. His greatness came through; he was named the Greatest First Baseman Ever in connection with the 1969 observance of baseball's centennial. He did, after all, hit .340 with 493 homers (the most ever by an American League first baseman), and he knocked in 1,991 runs (third all-time behind Hank Aaron and Babe Ruth).

Fate and the sportswriters were not always fair with Lou. He would hit .545 in a World Series, as he did in 1928, and the Bambino would come along and hit .625. Lou would become the first American Leaguer to hit four homers in one game, as he did on June 3, 1932, and that very day Giants' Manager John J. McGraw would announce his retirement and grab the headlines. Lou would hit two homers in a Series game, as he did in 1932, but it would be the game of Ruth's "called shot" home run and Lou's homers would get lost. The Baseball Writers would overlook Lou's Triple Crown 1934 season of .363, 49 homers, and 164 RBIs and give the MVP Award to Detroit's Mickey Cochrane, who hit .320 with two homers and 76 RBIs (while leading his team to the pennant, it might be added in fairness). Lou would not get his just due until he became ill in 1939.

Larrupin' Lou was born Henry Louis Gehrig on June 19, 1903, in New York City, the son of loving German immigrants. At Manhattan's Commerce High School, he was "the Babe Ruth of the high schools." At Columbia University, he was, by Yankee scout Paul Krichell's reckoning, "the next Babe Ruth." And when Lou, a solid 200-pounder with huge oak-tree legs, first joined the Yanks, he was "the Babe Ruth of the rookies."

Krichell signed Lou Gehrig in June of 1923, gave him a $1,500 bonus, and farmed him out to Hartford. The youngster had brief trials in New York, hitting .447 (17-for-38) over the combined 1923–24 seasons. He stuck with the Yankees in 1925, but warmed the bench and watched Wally Pipp play first base. On June 1, 1925, Gehrig pinch-hit for Pee Wee Wanninger. The next day Pipp rested with a headache. Manager Miller Huggins told Lou, "You're my first baseman today." Lou played that day and played and played for a big league record 2,130 consecutive games. The Iron Horse played with fractured fingers, charley horses, spike wounds, sore muscles, bad colds, lumbago, and back pains. He even played after a serious beaning.

Gehrig may have been the most consistent power hitter of all time. In each of his 13 complete seasons (1926–38), he drove in and scored 100 runs, an incredible major league record. In 1927, he drove home 175 runs, breaking Babe Ruth's American League record of 171 RBIs set in 1921. Then Lou broke his own record in 1931 with 184 RBIs, a still-standing league record. Gehrig led the league in RBIs five times and in runs scored four times.

Gehrig leads baseball's all-time grand-slam homer list with 23. In 1934, Larrupin' Lou hit 30 homers at home, the most in one season at Yankee Stadium. In 1936 he hit 14 homers against Cleveland alone. He won a piece of three home-run crowns. Perhaps the greatest compliment paid Lou was an indirect one by Josh Gibson, the Hall of Fame black star who patterned his hitting style after Gehrig's. Whenever possible, Gibson visited Yankee Stadium to study Lou, whose home-run total at the time of his 1939 retirement was exceeded by that of only one man: Babe Ruth.

But Gehrig was also a great contact hitter. He ranks first on the Yanks' all-time list for hits, extra-base hits, singles, doubles, and triples. Lou had eight 200-hit seasons—only Pete Rose and Ty Cobb have more. Gehrig homered 49 times in 1934 while striking out only 31 times. He hit .348, .308, .545, and .529 in his first four World Series.

Gehrig was no ballet dancer, but he got the job done around first base. He lacked speed but was no lumbering ox, either, although his slowness of foot might be more noticeable in today's game. He stole home 15 times and holds the Yankee club record for career thefts of home.

Gehrig was a decent, family-oriented homebody. As the perfect gentleman-ballplayer, Lou best exemplified the Yankee Image that Manager Joe McCarthy so carefully nurtured. He was made the Yankees' captain in 1935 and took the position seriously.

On May 2, 1939, Gehrig removed himself from the Yankee lineup, with his average at .143, and his playing streak ended. A few weeks later it was discovered that the source of Lou's slump was amyotrophic lateral sclerosis and that he had only two years to live. In July, Lou conceded he had been dealt a bad card but told a packed Yankee Stadium that he considered himself "the luckiest man on the face of the earth." The Yankees retired Lou's No. 4 uniform and he was ushered into the Baseball Hall of Fame by special election. On

LOU GEHRIG

June 2, 1941, 16 years to the day he replaced Wally Pipp, Lou Gehrig died. Sportswriter Al Mari some 40 years later would write, "Lou looked Death squarely in the eye and left this world with a smile on his face."

All-Star

Lou Gehrig was the American League's starting first baseman from 1933 through 1937, the first five years of the All-Star Game. He played in the 1938 game as a pinch-hitter. Lou had early difficulties, going a combined 0-for-9 over the first three games, but in the 1936 game at Boston's Braves Field, he put the Americans on the board with a seventh-inning solo homer off Curt Davis. However, the Nationals won, 4–3.

Gehrig was the hero of the 1937 game, hitting a homer and double, collecting four RBIs, and scoring a run in the Americans' 8–3 victory at Washington's Griffith Stadium. Lou broke up a 0–0 tie in the third inning with his two-run homer off Dizzy Dean. Dean tried to slip a fastball by Gehrig on a full count and Lou walloped it high and far over the distant right-field wall. Gehrig holds the record (53) for putouts by first basemen in All-Star Games.

Yankee Stats

	G	AB	R	H	2B	3B	HR	RBI	BA
17 Years	2,164	8,001	1,888	2,721	535	162	493	1,991	.340
7 World Series	34	119	30	43	8	3	10	35	.361
All-Star Games	6	18	4	4	1	0	2	5	.222

LEFTY GOMEZ

Career

The mythical Triple Crown of pitching, leading in wins, ERA, and strikeouts, has been won only 11 times in the American League, and Lefty Gomez won it twice, in 1934 and 1937. In the former season, he led the league in seven major categories. He led the league in strikeouts three times and is third on the Yanks' all-time strikeout list with 1,468. He is also third on the club's all-time win list with 189, trailing only Whitey Ford and Red Ruffing.

Vernon Louis Gomez was born in Rodeo, California, of Spanish-Irish descent on November 26, 1908. He pitched at Richmond High School in San Francisco and in his second year of professional baseball favorably impressed Yank scout Bill Essick. It was 1929 and Gomez was 18–11 with the San Francisco Seals. Essick urged the Yankees to obtain Gomez and they did, for $35,000.

Gomez began 1930 with the Yankees and ran his record to 2–5. He needed polish and work on his control. Baserunners were taking liberties on his high leg kick and he was sent down to St. Paul, where he learned to hold runners close and, generally, to be a more complete pitcher.

Returning to New York in 1931, Gomez posted a 21–9 record, followed by successive seasonal marks of 24–7, 16–10, and 26–5, his big 1934 season. In 1937, he won 20 games for the fourth time, going 21–11. This tied Bob Shawkey and Red Ruffing for the most 20-win seasons in Yankee history. Ruffing and Gomez, the Yankee pitching aces in the 1930s, formed one of the great righty-lefty combinations in history. The left side of the tandem was made great by "clean living and a fast outfield," according to Lefty.

Gomez in his prime was often compared with a 300-win contemporary, Lefty Grove. He was thin (6'2", 173 lbs), but he was a nail, and he had a whiplash arm. His explosive fastball belied his slight physique. Yankee General Manager Ed Barrow kept after Gomez to gain weight. Lefty did, then had a poor season. "Barrow told me that if I put on 20 pounds, I'd make the fans forget [Jack] Chesbro," he said. "I go Barrow three better with 23 pounds and almost make the fans forget Gomez."

In his great 1934 season, Gomez set the standing single-season Yankee record for left-handers with 26 wins, but he also injured his arm when his spikes caught on the mound. The ailing arm plagued him in 1935 and 1936 and Lefty was forced to become a finesse pitcher. He made the transition nicely, developing both an ability to fool hitters and a beautiful slow curveball. He had been a finisher— his 173 complete games is a Yankee record for left-handers—but late in his career Lefty appreciated Johnny Murphy's relief help.

Gomez was 12–8 in 1939, but his arm problems worsened and he slipped to 3–3 in 1940. He made a courageous comeback in 1941, going 15–5 for a league-leading .750 winning percentage. Once, late in Lefty's career, Bill Dickey asked him to try throwing harder."Throw harder?" asked Gomez."I'm throwing twice as hard as I ever did . . . It's just not getting there as fast!"

Gomez was a character. He was one of the most colorful players to ever wear pinstripes. The players, especially Babe Ruth, liked him immediately. Gomez befriended Joe DiMaggio and was the one teammate who could keep the shy DiMaggio laughing and loose."I've got a new invention," Gomez said one day. "It's a revolving bowl for tired goldfish." (Lefty had another nickname: "Goofy.") He greeted pigeons and was fascinated with flight. Manager Joe McCarthy, whom Lefty generally drove to despair, was less than amused that World Series day when pitcher Gomez, pausing to savor the flight of a passing plane, put a stutter in the action of the Fall Classic.

Gomez has the delightful ability to poke fun at himself. He likes to joke about a titanic home run that Jimmie Foxx hit off him. Years later (his sense of humor never fading) Lefty joked, "When Neil Armstrong first set foot on the moon, he and all the space scientists were puzzled by an unidentifiable white object. I knew immediately what it was. That was a home run hit off me in 1937 by Jimmie Foxx."

But Lefty Gomez would get down to business in October. He was 6–0 in World Series play, the most wins without a loss in history. And his first five wins were complete games. Lefty beat the New York Giants four times over the 1936 and 1937 World Series.

The one thing Lefty couldn't do was hit, as his .147 lifetime average attests. Ruth and others watched in amusement as Lefty practiced hitting. Yet Lefty could take pride in two plate accomplishments in the 1937 World Series. In the opener, he drew two walks in one inning. In the finale, he singled in the winning run.

The Yankees sold Gomez' contract to the Boston Braves in January of 1943, but Lefty never got into a Braves game. He did pitch (and lose) one game for Washington before his retirement. Later he returned to the Yankees as a minor league manager and coach.

All-Star

Lefty Gomez was probably the most successful pitcher in the history of the All-Star Game. He was picked to every American League team from 1933 through 1939 and started games in 1933, 1934, 1935, 1937, and 1938, a record five starts, later tied by National Leaguers Robin Roberts and Don Drysdale. Gomez won three games, a record he alone holds.

In the 1933 game, the first in All-Star history, Lefty blanked the Nationals on two hits in three innings to gain credit for the Americans' 4–2 win. He also knocked in the first run in All-Star competition on a solid second-inning single.

Gomez went the first six innings, the longest stint in All-Star competition, in the 1935 game. He allowed only three hits and one run, getting credit for the Americans' 4–1 win. He one-hit the Nationals over the first three innings of the 1937 game and got credit for the 8–3 American League victory. In the 1938 game, he gave up only one unearned run in the first three innings but took a hardluck defeat. Lefty was the American League's honorary captain for the 1979 game.

Yankee Stats

	W	L	PCT	G	GS	CG	SA	SO	ERA
13 Years	189	101	.652	367	319	173	9	1,468	3.34
5 World Series	6	0	1.000	7	7	4	0	31	2.86
All-Star Games	3	1	.750	5	5	0	0	9	2.50

LEFTY GOMEZ

JOE GORDON

Career

Joe "Flash" Gordon played in exactly 1,000 Yankee games and made exactly 1,000 hits. The successor to the great Tony Lazzeri and the barter for the great Allie Reynolds, Gordon himself was an outstanding Yankee at the plate and in the field. He was the premier second baseman in the American League for a decade.

Gordon, a native of Los Angeles who played high school baseball in Portland, Oregon, was signed out of the University of Oregon, where he hit .418, by Yankee scout Bill Essick. A slick-fielding shortstop, Gordon was switched to second base and was groomed to replace the aging Lazzeri. He hit .280 with 26 homers at Newark in 1937.

Following the 1937 season, Gordon was asked if recent news that he would replace the legendary Lazzeri unnerved him. "No, I was rather pleased," said Joe, who never lacked for confidence or honesty. The next spring Manager Joe McCarthy was ecstatic about his new, flashy, double-play combination of Gordon and shortstop Frank Crosetti. But the 23-year-old rookie Gordon began the 1938 season slowly and was benched for a while. He then got on track and finished with 25 home runs and 97 RBIs in 127 games. In the World Series sweep of the Cubs, Flash batted .400.

Gordon was the Yanks' regular second sacker through the 1943 season, except for a brief experiment in 1941 when he played 30 games at first base. He had fast hands, quick feet, and was an acrobatic second baseman who turned the double play beautifully and covered a lot of ground. Three times as a Yankee he led the league's second basemen in assists and double plays.

Gordon hit 253 homers (153 with New York and 100 with Cleveland), the most in league history by a second baseman. He hit 20-plus homers in each of his first four seasons, including 30 in 1940. But Joe didn't just hit for power. He hit .500 in the 1941 World Series and in 1942 he hit safely in 29 consecutive games.

He was the league MVP in 1942, the year he hit his career high of .322, but it was probably not his best season. Joe, a right-handed hitter, hit 18 homers and collected 103 RBIs; he also led the league in strikeouts and hit into the most double plays. Moreover, he led second basemen in errors.

After missing the 1944 and 1945 seasons because of military service, Gordon returned to second base in 1946 and hit only .210 in 112 games. Rustiness and injuries conspired to hurt his performance. There were reports that he didn't get along with his new manager, Bill Dickey, but Gordon denied these. However, he never denied that he had difficulties with Yankee President Larry MacPhail, who in October of 1946 traded Joe to Cleveland for Allie Reynolds. Gordon gave the Tribe four excellent years, including a 124-RBI performance in 1948.

All-Star

Joe Gordon was an All-Star in six Yankee seasons, every season except his rookie year of 1938, and got into three more games as an Indian. He was 0-for-10 at bat as a starter in 1939, 1940, and 1942. As a substitute in the 1941 game, Gordon came through with a key single and scored a run in the Americans' four-run ninth-inning rally, as the junior circuit won, 7–5, in Detroit. He got a two-bagger and knocked in two runs as a sub in the 1946 game.

Yankee Stats

	G	AB	R	H	2B	3B	HR	RBI	BA
7 Years	1,000	3,686	596	1,000	186	38	153	617	.271
5 World Series	23	81	9	21	5	1	3	14	.259
All-Star Games	5	14	1	2	1	0	0	2	.143

JOE GORDON

RICH GOSSAGE

Career

Off the baseball diamond, Rich "Goose" Gossage is a mild-mannered, soft-spoken gentleman. On the mound he is a raging bull, scowling at intimidated batters and blowing fastballs by them. Few hitters care to dig in against Goose, whose fastball was clocked (in 1980) at 99.4 mph. Gossage is "The Exorcist," Richie Zisk explains, "because he scares the devil out of you."

The 6'3", 215-pound native of Colorado Springs, Colorado, issues from an all-arms-and-legs delivery a fastball that hops and sails and darts. When he can paint the black of the plate with it, he is all but impossible to hit. And the Goose has a hard, breaking ball (a slurve) that freezes right-handed hitters. Tough to hit? In his first five Yankee seasons (1978–82), Gossage struck out 416 batters in 431 innings.

Gossage broke into the majors with the White Sox in 1972 and was coming off a 26-save season with Pittsburgh in 1977 when the Yankees signed the 26-year-old free agent to a lucrative six-year contract.

Sharing the Yankee bullpen with Sparky Lyle in 1978, the big right-hander led the league in saves with 27. He capped off a great year by saving the division playoff game at Boston, the final game of the Championship Series against Kansas City, and the finale of the World Series against Los Angeles. The playoff at Fenway Park was particularly dramatic, the Goose retiring Jim Rice and Carl Yastrzemski to end the game with the tying and winning runs on base.

After being disabled from April 21 to July 9 in 1979 (yet managing to save 18 games), in 1980 Gossage enjoyed his greatest season and was the difference between the first-place Yankees and the chasing Orioles. Goose set the Yankee record for most saves by a right-hander with 33, tying Dan Quisenberry for the league lead. He saved 33 games in 37 possible save situations and was 25-for-25 at one point. He saved 17 late-season games (after August 15), retiring 28 consecutive batters in one seven-game stretch.

Before the Great Baseball Strike interrupted play in 1981, Goose recorded 17 saves in 18 possible save situations. He finished with 20 saves and an 0.77 ERA, although he had assorted back, shoulder, and groin injuries. He was awesome in the postseason, saving two games apiece against the Brewers, A's, and Dodgers. Goose didn't allow a single run in his entire eight-game, 14-inning, postseason performance.

Gossage had only the third 30-save season in Yankee history (Rich owns two) in 1982. He fanned 102 batters in 93 innings and held hitters to a .196 average, accomplishing this in spite of a sore pitching shoulder that had him sidelined for a month.

Through 1982, Gossage had 128 saves as a Yankee, placing him second to Sparky Lyle's 141 on New York's all-time list. But Goose has already earned the right to be called the greatest relief pitcher in Yankee history. No one in baseball history has ever done his job better than Rich Gossage has done his.

All-Star

Rich Gossage was an All-Star with two teams before joining the Yankees. As a Yankee, he was an All-Star in 1978, 1980, 1981, and 1982, although he was forced to miss the 1981 game because of shoulder tightness. He pitched in the 1978 and 1980 games, taking the loss in 1978.

Yankee Stats

	W	L	PCT	G	GS	CG	SA	SO	ERA
5 Years	28	23	.549	251	0	0	128	416	2.07
3 Champ. Series	1	1	.500	5	0	0	3	5	5.14
2 World Series	1	0	1.000	6	0	0	2	9	0.00
All-Star Games	0	1	.000	2	0	0	0	1	18.00

RICH GOSSAGE (©1981 Janice E. Rettaliata)

BOB GRIM

Career

Bob Grim came out of nowhere in 1954 to win 20 games and the American League's Rookie of the Year Award. Although he broke into the Yankee organization six years earlier, he spent the previous year in the military, and was not even on the Yanks' 1954 spring training roster. Yet he impressed Manager Casey Stengel and stuck with the big club.

A native New Yorker who preferred a little fishing to big city life, Grim was the first Yankee rookie to win 20 games since Russ Ford (1910). No Yankee rookie has since won 20. His record was 20–6 and he was 8–0 in relief. The 24-year-old right-hander was New York's top winner and, having pitched only 199 innings, remains the only 20-game winner in history to have pitched fewer than 200 innings.

Grim was an uncomplicated pitcher who came right at hitters with his good fastball and slider. Arm troubles complicated things for him, however; he first experienced them in 1955 and they haunted his career. Unable to go more than three or four innings at a time, he became a relief pitcher and in 1957 led the league in both saves (19) and relief wins (12). But then he incurred more arm problems and lost his slider, so the Yankees traded him to Kansas City in June of 1958. Bob finished in 1962 with a career mark of 61–41.

All-Star

Bob Grim was a member of the 1957 All-Stars and saved a 6–5 American League win at St. Louis' Busch Stadium. After the Nationals rallied for three runs in the bottom of the ninth, Casey Stengel summoned Grim, who retired Gil Hodges to end the game.

Yankee Stats

	W	L	PCT	G	GS	CG	SA	SO	ERA
5 Years	45	21	.682	146	37	10	28	282	3.35
2 World Series	0	2	.000	5	1	0	1	10	4.91
All-Star Games	0	0	.000	1	0	0	1	0	0.00

BOB GRIM

RON GUIDRY

Career

Ron Guidry was discouraged. After years of bouncing around the minors and a 1976 season of shuttling between New York and Syracuse, Guidry was so discouraged that he seriously considered quitting baseball. But his wife, Bonnie, urged him to give it one more try—the rest is history.

Born August 28, 1950, in Lafayette, Louisiana, Guidry was a track star in high school and a pitcher for the University of Southwestern Louisiana. Scout Atley Donald, a Yankee pitcher from 1938 through 1945, was impressed with Guidry's athletic abilities and made him the Yanks' third pick in the June 1971 amateur draft.

The Yankees decided to make a relief pitcher of Guidry, whose speed and strong arm might have taken him to the majors as an outfielder. He began at Johnson City in 1971, worked in three other towns, and reached Syracuse in 1975. The Yanks called him up in 1975 and Ron got into 10 games, starting one. In 1976, Ron made only seven relief appearances for New York (0–0, 16 innings, 5.63 ERA), and his career as a relief pitcher appeared stymied even though he was 5–1 with an 0.68 ERA in Syracuse.

He made the Yankees in the spring of 1977 but saw little early-season action as a reliever. When several starters were taken out by injuries, Ron was handed a place in the starting rotation. He finished 16–7, tying Ed Figueroa for the club leadership in victories. He began a phenomenal 37–4 streak on August 10 that extended through postseason play and 1978. He capped 1977 with two postseason triumphs, a three-hitter against the Royals and a four-hitter against the Dodgers.

Louisiana Lightning, as the fans call Guidry, enjoyed a storybook season in 1978. In 35 starts, he was 25–3, with seven no-decisions, and he was the unanimous winner of the Cy Young Award. In 1978, Ron:

- Led the league with 25 wins, the most by a Yankee since Whitey Ford's 25 in 1961.
- Won his first 13 decisions, setting a new club record for most consecutive wins at the start of the season, formerly held by Atley Donald, who won his first 12 in 1939.
- Established a major league record for highest winning percentage, .893, among 20-game winners.

- Led the league with nine shutouts, tying Babe Ruth's 1916 record (when Ruth was with Boston) for the most shutouts by a left-hander in American League history.
- Led the league with a 1.74 ERA, the lowest ERA by a left-handed starter in Yankee history.
- Set a Yankee strikeout record with 248, breaking Jack Chesbro's 1904 record of 239 whiffs, and set a single-game league record for left-handers by fanning 18 Angels on June 17.
- Beat Boston in the divisional playoff, Kansas City in the pennant clincher, and Los Angeles in the World Series (with New York down two games to none).

RON GUIDRY (NY Yankees)

Guidry has not matched his 1978 season since—no one has—but he has been excellent. He was 18–8 in 1979 and won his second straight ERA title with 2.78. The next season he won his first six decisions, had a mid-season slump, then took his final four to finish at 17–10. He went 11–5 in 1981 and had the best strikeout-to-walk ratio in the majors. He won the 1981 World Series opener and lost a tough 2–1 decision to the Dodgers in Game 5, his first Series loss. After running his 1982 record to 8–1 on June 14, Ron was unable to win again until July 18. He finished at 14–8.

When he captured his 100th win on August 31, 1982, Ron's winning percentage of .719 (100–39) put him at the top of the class among baseball's 100-game winners. By the season's close, his winning percentage dropped to .706, which ranks him second in Yankee history behind Spud Chandler. Ron has a career losing record against only Baltimore (5–6) and California (4–5); he has beaten Detroit most often (13–4). Louisiana Lightning ranks sixth in strikeouts and seventh in ERA on Yankee lists through 1982.

His smallish size (5′11″, 162 lbs) aside, Guidry produces a 95 mph fastball, which, combined with his hard, dipping slider, makes Gator devastatingly effective for seven innings. In recent years, Guidry has added a good change-up and doesn't try to overpower every hitter. He now will let hitters get themselves out. Ron is a great chess player both on and off the field. But his athletic ability is his strong suit. He won a Gold Glove in 1982 as the league's best fielding pitcher.

Whatever the future may hold for Ron Guidry, Yankee fans won't forget his past. No single Yankee contributed more to the Yanks' 1977 and 1978 World Championships than did Ron Guidry, a class act off the field as well as on.

All-Star

Ron Guidry was a member of the American League's pitching staff for the 1978, 1979, and 1982 All-Star Games. He pitched only 1/3 of an inning each in the 1978 and 1979 games, garnering no decisions, and wasn't used in the 1982 game.

Yankee Stats

	W	L	PCT	G	GS	CG	SA	SO	ERA
8 Years	101	42	.706	210	174	51	4	1,084	2.91
5 Champ. Series	2	1	.667	5	4	1	0	17	4.03
3 World Series	3	1	.750	4	4	2	0	26	1.69
All-Star Games	0	0	.000	2	0	0	0	0	0.00

ROLLIE HEMSLEY

Career

The Yankees were in a bind in July of 1942. First-string catcher Bill Dickey was hurt and backup Buddy Rosar, pursuing personal matters, made himself unavailable. So the Yanks signed veteran catcher Rollie Hemsley, who after hitting .113 in 36 games had been released by Cincinnati.

Hemsley broke into the majors in 1928 and was a much traveled and highly respected defensive backstop. The native of Syracuse, Ohio, was sometimes called Rollicking Rollie. "Rollie could catch drunk better than most guys could sober," Bob Feller once said.

The day Hemsley joined the Yankees, he caught both ends of a doubleheader in oppressive heat and nearly fainted from exhaustion. But he was valuable, hitting .294 in 31 Yankee games. Two years later, in 1944, Hemsley was splitting the catching chores with Mike Garbark and hitting .268 in 81 games when he became a 37-year-old sailor with the U. S. Navy.

Hemsley caught 1,495 games in his career to rank in baseball's top 20. Coincidentally, his Yankee career average of .262 matches his lifetime average for 19 seasons in the majors.

All-Star

Rollie Hemsley played in the 1935 All-Star Game as a Brown and in the 1940 game as an Indian. In 1944, as a Yankee, he was the starting catcher and went hitless in two trips. The Nationals won, 7–1, in Pittsburgh.

Yankee Stats

	G	AB	R	H	2B	3B	HR	RBI	BA
3 Years	174	549	47	144	21	9	4	65	.262
All-Star Games	1	2	0	0	0	0	0	0	.000

ROLLIE HEMSLEY

TOMMY HENRICH

Career

Born February 20, 1913, Tommy Henrich grew up playing baseball every chance he got in his hometown of Massillon, Ohio. He broke into the Cleveland organization in 1934, had three splendid seasons in the minors, and became convinced that the Indians for reasons of their own were keeping him out of the majors. Commissioner Landis thought so, too, and declared Henrich a free agent. The Yankees signed the young outfielder for a $25,000 bonus in April of 1937.

Henrich impressed Manager Joe McCarthy but found himself at Newark. He hit .440 (11-for-25) for the Bears and was called up to the Yankees where he belonged. The boyish-looking, left-handed Henrich batted .320 in 67 games as a Yankee in 1937 and had a starting job with the big club in 1938.

Henrich, Joe DiMaggio, and Charlie Keller formed one of the greatest outfields in baseball history. They peaked in their home-run hitting in 1941, when Keller hit 33, Henrich 31, and DiMaggio 30. Four times in his career Tommy broke the 20-homer mark. In 1947 and 1948, he led the league in triples. His best season at the plate was 1948 when he hit .308 with 42 doubles, 14 triples, and 25 homers, had 100 RBIs and scored a league-leading 138 runs.

Nicknamed "Old Reliable" by broadcaster Mel Allen, Henrich, a mentally tough player, was one of the best clutch hitters in Yankee history. He hit four homers with the bases loaded in 1948, tying an American League record (later broken by Baltimore's Jim Gentile). In the opening game of the 1949 World Series, Tommy broke up a scoreless tie with a home run in the bottom of the ninth inning off Brooklyn's Don Newcombe.

Henrich made his plate appearances count. Through 1982, he remains in the top 10 on New York's all-time lists for triples, walks, homers, and RBIs. Yet Tommy is not in the top 20 for at bats.

Henrich was just as reliable in the field, where he roamed with an intelligence all his own. He was an aggressive right fielder who charged base hits and fired his throws, sometimes nailing inattentive runners who rounded first base too far. Another favorite play of Tommy's was to trap a fly ball and force a faster runner already on base. He studied hitters and practiced taking rebounds off the tricky walls at Yankee Stadium. "Catching the ball is a pleasure," said Tommy. "Knowing what to do with it is a business." Tommy also played

TOMMY HENRICH (NY Yankees)

at first base (189 games) late in his career and did an outstanding job.

"I get a thrill every time I put on my Yankee uniform," said Henrich, whose loyalty to the Yankees, combined with his special enthusiasm and love of the game, made him conspicuously popular with Yankee fans. On August 30, 1942, a Stadium announcer told a large Sunday crowd that Tommy was leaving the club to join the Coast Guard; Tommy received one of the greatest ovations in Yankee Stadium history.

Henrich missed three full seasons, but returned a more productive player in 1946. Arthritic knees forced his retirement after the 1950 season. Henrich, who helped the Yankees win seven World Championships, remained with the Yankees as a coach in 1951.

All-Star

Tommy Henrich was a five-time All-Star, making the American League team in 1942 and 1947–50. In the 1942 game, Tommy started in right field and got a key double off Mort Cooper and scored in the Americans' three-run first inning, as they held on to win, 3–1, at the Polo Grounds. Henrich replaced the injured Ted Williams in left field as a starter in the 1948 game, going hitless in three trips. Tommy didn't play in 1949.

Yankee Stats

	G	AB	R	H	2B	3B	HR	RBI	BA
11 Years	1,284	4,603	901	1,297	269	73	183	795	.282
4 World Series	21	84	13	22	4	0	4	8	.262
All-Star Games	4	9	1	1	1	0	0	0	.111

ELSTON HOWARD

Career

Elston Howard will always be remembered for breaking racial barriers. He was the first black Yankee, the first black MVP in the American League, and the first black coach in the American League. But to remember Howard chiefly as a racial wedge, however important his contributions as such may have been, disserves his gifts as a truly outstanding ballplayer and, above all else, a wonderful human being.

The Yankees bought Howard's contract in 1950 from the Kansas City Monarchs, a team in the old Negro Leagues. Ellie served in the military in 1951 and 1952, and entered the minors. In 1954, in his first full season as a catcher, Ellie was the MVP of the International League, hitting .330 with Toronto. The next season the St. Louis-born Howard was a 26-year-old Yankee rookie.

Howard was treated like a second-class citizen in the spring of 1955, forced to live in a segregated section of St. Petersburg, Florida, because of a policy at the hotel where the Yankees were lodged. Howard never accepted his status, but he was too much of a gentleman to make an issue. Soft-spoken and well-educated, Ellie worried more about his job on the field. His Yankee teammates warmly accepted him and Manager Casey Stengel always praised Howard for his baseball ability and competitive spirit.

Stengel called Howard his "three-way platoon." In his first five seasons, Ellie was without a regular position. He was Yogi Berra's backup catcher, he played in the outfield, and he played first base. Finally, in 1960, Ellie took over the bulk of the catching load and held a regular job through the 1966 season. Ellie was the best all-round catcher in the 1960s.

Howard's career really took off when Ralph Houk became manager in 1961, the year Ellie hit .348 in 446 at bats, including a .405 average against left-handers. In 1962, Ellie had 91 RBIs, his career high, including eight in one game on August 19. In 1963, he had a career-high 28 home runs and was the league's MVP. Howard topped .300 for the third time at .313 in 1964 and drove in the winning run in 21 games.

Only three right-handed hitters have hit more Yankee home runs than Ellie's 161—Joe DiMaggio (361), Tony Lazzeri (169), and Bill Skowron (165). Howard had good power to all fields and parked many

ELSTON HOWARD (NY Yankees)

four-baggers into the right field porch at Yankee Stadium. He had immense hands and strong wrists.

As a catcher, Howard had few peers. He gave a pitching staff confidence. He won the Gold Glove in 1963 and 1964, the latter year setting the Yankee record for catchers with a .998 fielding average. His lifetime mark of .993 is the second highest in baseball history among retired catchers.

The Yankees won the pennant in nine of Howard's first 10 seasons as a Yankee. Yogi Berra and Mickey Mantle are the only players in history with more World Series games played than Howard's 54. Ellie hit a homer in his first World Series trip to the plate in the 1955 Series. He won the Babe Ruth Award in the 1958 Series, making a tremendous catch in left field at a key time in Game 5 and driving in the winning run in Game 7. He led all hitters with a .462 average in the 1960 Series.

Injuries plagued Ellie late in his career and, with his average at .196 in August of 1967, the Yanks dealt him to Boston, where Ellie helped the Red Sox win a pennant. He returned to the Yankees as a coach in 1969, moving into the Yankee front office in 1980. Elston Howard died of heart failure on December 14, 1980, and the Yankees lost a first-class citizen.

All-Star

Elston Howard was an All-Star for nine consecutive years (1957–65), but saw little action. He didn't play in his first game until 1960 and didn't start until 1964. In the 1964 game, played at Shea Stadium, Ellie, after going hitless in three trips, was hit by a pitch and eventually scored the tying run in the seventh inning. But the Nationals broke the tie and won, 7–4.

Yankee Stats

	G	AB	R	H	2B	3B	HR	RBI	BA
13 Years	1,492	5,044	588	1,405	211	50	161	733	.279
9 World Series	47	153	25	40	7	1	5	18	.261
All-Star Games	6	9	1	0	0	0	0	0	.000

CATFISH HUNTER

Career

Two great comeback stories unfolded in 1978. The Yankees came from 14 games back to win the American League East title, and Catfish Hunter, who, disabled for much of the season, won 10 of his final 13 decisions to finish at 12-6. Hunter's great second half was the single biggest factor in New York's overtaking frontrunning Boston. The road to recovery began in July, when he had his aching pitching shoulder manipulated to break down adhesions, continued through a 6-0 August, and ended in the finale of the World Series, when Hunter pitched seven strong innings and beat the Dodgers.

James Augustus Hunter was born April 8, 1946, in Hertford, North Carolina. He never played in the minor leagues, breaking in with the Kansas City A's in 1965. He pitched a perfect game for the Oakland A's in 1968 and, beginning in 1971, he was a 20-game winner four years in a row. But after the 1974 season, Hunter was declared a free agent by an arbitration panel that ruled A's owner Charles O. Finley had reneged on certain contractual obligations due Hunter. On December 31, 1974, Hunter signed a historic five-year contract with the Yankees, making him by far the highest-paid player in baseball history.

Hunter displayed true class in the spring of 1975, patiently giving interview after interview. Yankee fans loved him right away, as did his teammates. Catfish had a great year, going 23-14 to tie Jim Palmer for the league lead in wins and joining Walter Johnson and Lefty Grove as the only American League 20-game winners in five consecutive years. Catfish also led the league with 30 complete games and 328 innings pitched, the most in either category by a Yankee pitcher since Carl Mays had 30 and 337 in 1921. The maximum Hunter could have pitched if he had finished all 39 starts is 346 innings. Some believe his heavy workload in 1975 led to his later arm problems. The record shows he pitched progressively fewer innings each year as a Yankee.

Hunter was 17-15 in 299 innings pitched in 1976 and won the opener of the Championship Series against the Royals. The following Opening Day, Catfish was hit by a line drive to begin a season plagued by injuries and arm ailments. Then came his great comeback in 1978. He retired gracefully after the 1979 season and returned to North Carolina to a life of farming, hunting, and fishing.

CATFISH HUNTER (AP Laser Photo — 1978)

Based largely on his 224–166 lifetime record, Hunter seems a cinch for the Baseball Hall of Fame. He was an artist on the mound, painting the black of the plate, moving the ball around, and keeping batters off stride. "I always said my best pitch was my 'control,'" said Catfish, who also worked quickly. He let hitters get themselves out, and although he allowed the most homers (374) in league history, Catfish ranks in the top 20 in history for allowing the fewest baserunners per nine innings (10.20).

All-Star

Catfish Hunter was an eight-time All-Star, including selection to the 1975 and 1976 junior circuit teams as a Yankee. He pitched in four games as an Athletic, taking a tough loss in the 1967 game. In the 1975 game played in Milwaukee, Hunter was charged with two runs in the ninth inning and took the loss, as the Nationals broke a 3–3 tie and won, 6–3. In the 1976 game, Hunter again allowed two runs in two innings, but he also struck out Johnny Bench, Dave Kingman, and Tom Seaver.

Yankee Stats

	W	L	PCT	G	GS	CG	SA	SO	ERA
5 Years	63	53	.543	137	136	65	0	492	3.58
2 Champ. Series	1	1	.500	3	3	1	0	10	4.50
3 World Series	1	3	.250	5	4	1	0	11	4.85
All-Star Games	0	1	.000	2	0	0	0	5	9.00

REGGIE JACKSON

Career

"Reggie! Reggie! Reggie!" the Yankee Stadium crowd chanted as Reginald Martinez Jackson ran out his third home run of the evening against Los Angeles. It was the final game of the 1977 World Series and Jackson had joined Babe Ruth as the only players to hit three homers in one World Series game. One of the great pressure players in history, a man worthy of the moniker, "Mr. October," Reggie had led the Yankees to their first World Championship in 15 years and the next day would be the toast of Manhattan in a riotous ticker-tape parade. It was Jackson's greatest hour and it ended one of the most bizarre seasons ever.

Jackson, a native of Wyncote, Pennsylvania, was one of the game's premier performers ever since joining the Kansas City A's in 1967. In November of 1976, Reggie was the biggest name in the first free agent reentry draft and not long thereafter signed a five-year contract for close to three million dollars to play for the Yankees.

The 31-year-old Jackson spent 1977 in a fish bowl as the Yankees led baseball through the uncharted waters of free agency. No established star since Babe Ruth became a Yankee in 1920 had joined a club with as much commotion as surrounded Reggie in 1977.

Most clubs and fans were against free agency and Jackson weathered hostile reactions, especially in the blue-collar cities around the circuit. That "New York" was written across Reggie's chest didn't help the situation. But Reggie alienated many of his own New York fans, first by making foolish statements that degraded Thurman Munson and then by nearly coming to blows with Manager Billy Martin in front of a national TV audience. Through all Reggie's conflicts with his teammates, his manager, the fans, and the press, he still belted 32 homers with 110 RBIs, and vindicated owner George Steinbrenner, who had signed Jackson and who stuck by Reggie all year.

The Steinbrenner-Jackson relationship would eventually cool, but the Martin-Jackson relationship heated up again in July of 1978, when Reggie was suspended for bunting against his manager's orders. Still, Reggie hit 27 home runs with 97 RBIs and was a vital cog in the Yanks' drive to the 1978 World Championship. In the 11 postseason games against Boston, Kansas City, and Los Angeles, Jackson hit a combined .400 with five homers and 15 RBIs.

Jackson enjoyed his best Yankee season in 1980, hitting 41 homers to share the home run crown with Ben Oglivie and driving in 111 runs. He hit 10 homers in July, many of them game winners, and belted his 400th career homer in August. After a late-summer slump, he hit safely in the final 13 games and poled a home run to clinch the division title on October 4.

Reggie entered into contract talks with Steinbrenner in 1981, but these broke down early in the spring and never resumed. Jackson played most of the season as if in a coma and was hitting .199 when the baseball strike interrupted play in June. He needed an exceptional September to finish at .237 with 15 homers and 54 RBIs. He didn't look like a million-dollar ballplayer in 1981, but he had one more clutch hit to deliver in pinstripes: In the fifth and deciding game of the division series, with New York trailing Milwaukee, 2–0, he crunched a two-run homer and the Yanks went on to rout the Brewers.

Following the 1981 season, Jackson became a free agent for the second time and signed a million-dollar-a-year contract (plus attendance clauses) with the Angels, a team he had been eying for some time. He had a splendid 1982 season for Gene Autry, hitting 39 homers with 101 RBIs.

Evaluating Jackson as a ballplayer has been a favorite pastime with fans. His detractors point to Reggie's fielding, but Jackson made some great catches in the clutch for the Yankees. He never hit .300, others say, but Reggie wiped away that argument in 1980 by hitting .300 on the nose. He strikes out too much, some contend. Reggie is the game's all-time strikeout king and is "improving" on his record with each game. But he is a consistent power hitter, belting 20 or more homers in 13 consecutive seasons (1968–80), and only the Strike of 1981 has kept it from being 15 seasons. In World Series play, Reggie has the top slugging average in history at .755. It is his great postseason performances that have made him so visible. Thus, the more casual fan tends to put Reggie in the class of Hank Aaron, Willie Mays, and Mickey Mantle, where he doesn't belong. By the same token, many knowledgeable fans tend to underrate Jackson, sniping at the imperfections that keep him from being one of the great all-round players. There is no denying that Reggie is headed for the Baseball Hall of Fame. Jackson is a winner, having played on five World Championship clubs.

All-Star

Before joining the Yankees, Reggie Jackson was an All-Star in 1969 and 1971–75. His most memorable moment came in the 1971 game when he walloped a home run off the light tower above the right-field roof at Tiger Stadium. Reggie was an All-Star in each of his five years with the Yankees and was voted a starter in 1977, 1978, 1980, and 1981, although he missed the 1978 game with an injury. Reggie delivered a single in two at bats in the 1977 game played at Yankee Stadium, and was an All-Star as an Angel in 1982.

Yankee Stats

	G	AB	R	H	2B	3B	HR	RBI	BA
5 Years	653	2,349	380	661	115	14	144	461	.281
4 Champ. Series	14	44	8	11	2	0	2	8	.250
3 World Series	15	55	15	22	3	0	8	17	.400
All-Star Games	4	6	0	2	0	0	0	0	.333

REGGIE JACKSON (NY Yankees)

TOMMY JOHN

Career

Tommy John has the ability to make sluggers look like potato sacks. His philosophy is simple: "I was always taught that the art of pitching was to throw as close to the plate as possible without it being a strike."

The southpaw has a good curveball and a sneaky fastball, but his best pitch is his bionic sinkerball, which entices hitters into beating weak grounders to infielders. Clyde King calls John "an adjuster," meaning that if his sinker isn't working, he will adjust—go to another pitch and maybe come back to the sinker later. Others maintain that John is a master at doctoring the ball by cutting it. This reputation alone gives Tommy a psychological edge over batters. He is efficient, too. In a 1980 win against Seattle, John used only 81 pitches. Earlier in his career, he pitched a complete game with only 72 pitches.

John wasn't always a finesse pitcher. He reached the majors with Cleveland in 1963 as a fireballing power pitcher. He later pitched for the White Sox and Dodgers. Then, in 1974, he suffered what seemed to be irreparable damage to his pitching elbow. He underwent repair that required the transplant of a tendon taken from his right arm. With his "reconstructed" left arm (the Bionic Arm), John made a great comeback with the Dodgers in 1976, but when the club refused his contract demands, he became a free agent and signed with the Yankees in November of 1978.

Born in Terre Haute, Indiana, on May 22, 1943, John is the epitome of the conservative Midwesterner—a cleancut model citizen and a faithful family man. He is religious and patriotic, and all these qualities were highly visible in his Yankee career.

John started 1979 with nine consecutive wins and finished at 21–9. The next year he won his first seven decisions, finished at 22–9 and led the league in shutouts with six. In 1981, John was a hard-luck 9–8, and New York scored only 12 runs in his defeats, but won two Opening Days—the season starter and the opener of the so-called Second Season, the post-strike portion of 1981. In the World Series against the Dodgers, Tommy allowed only one earned run and didn't walk a batter in 13 innings.

Through 1981, John enjoyed a close relationship with George Steinbrenner and often publicly praised the Yankee owner. But the relationship fell apart in 1982. In February, John nearly took the Yankees to arbitration before accepting an extra year on his contract.

Then he pitched poorly and, in late July, Manager Gene Michael sent him to the bullpen. John announced that he wanted to be traded, but only to Boston, Milwaukee, Kansas City, or California. John publicly found fault with the Yankee front office, too. He rallied to improve his record to 10–10, but on August 31 the Yankees made John a happy man and dealt him to the Angels.

All-Star
Before joining the Yankees, Tommy John was a member of the American League team in 1968 and the National League team in 1978. As a Yankee, he was twice selected as an All-Star. He didn't get to play in 1979, and in the 1980 game, Tommy took the loss at Dodger Stadium, allowing three runs, including a Ken Griffey homer, in 2 1/3 innings of work.

Yankee Stats

	W	L	PCT	G	GS	CG	SA	SO	ERA
4 Years	62	36	.633	123	118	49	0	293	3.20
2 Champ. Series	6	1	0	1.000	2	2	0	0	2.13
1 World Series	1	0	1.000	3	2	0	0	8	0.69
All-Star Games	0	1	.000	1	0	0	0	1	11.57

TOMMY JOHN (NY Yankees)

BILLY JOHNSON

Career

Billy Johnson is one of those fine players who, on the Yankees, sometimes gets lost among the great names. Johnson was born August 30, 1918, in Montclair, New Jersey, and signed with the Yankees for $100 in 1937. Six sweat-filled years later he moved up to the Yanks from Newark and went to work for Manager Joe McCarthy. Johnson was only 5'9", but he had a strong, compact build and was known as "the Bull." In his rookie year of 1943, he played third base in every one of the Yanks' 155 games, knocking in 94 runs. Defensively, he led league third basemen in putouts, assists, and double plays. He hit .300 in the World Series victory over the Cardinals, delivering the Classic's most important hit, an eight-inning bases-loaded triple that wiped out a one-run Yankee deficit in Game 3.

Returning from a two-year hitch in the army, in 1946 Johnson found his circumstances changed with McCarthy gone. The Bull was no longer first-string. But when Bobby Brown broke a finger in May of 1947, Johnson stepped in and had a great year, his 95 RBIs standing as the club record for third basemen until Graig Nettles had 107 in 1977. In the Yanks' seven-game World Series triumph over Brooklyn, Billy hit three triples and scored eight runs.

Johnson was first-string in 1948 for the second year under Manager Bucky Harris and had a career-high .294 batting average. He was a steady, solid hitter and an excellent defender of the hot corner, and he had a rifle arm. But another new manager, Casey Stengel, was wary of his lack of speed and propensity for hitting into double plays. In 1949 and 1950, Stengel platooned the right-handed-hitting Johnson with the left-handed-hitting Brown. Johnson's career was stunted and in May of 1951 the Yankees dealt him to the Cardinals. Two years later, Billy's big league career ended. He is remembered as a valuable member of four championship clubs.

All-Star

Billy Johnson was an All-Star in 1947. He went into the game late as a defensive replacement for Detroit's George Kell, the starting third baseman. Billy didn't get to bat in the game at Wrigley Field. The Americans won, 2–1.

Yankee Stats

	G	AB	R	H	2B	3B	HR	RBI	BA
7 Years	735	2,524	344	694	107	30	45	388	.275
4 World Series	18	59	11	14	1	4	0	5	.237
All-Star Games	1	0	0	0	0	0	0	0	.000

BILLY JOHNSON (NY Yankees)

CHARLIE KELLER

Career

Charlie Keller was one of the strongest players of his time. The intimidating slugger was known to fans as "King Kong" and "Killer Keller." Professionally, he was an intense all-out player, a perfectionist who always felt he should be doing better. But he didn't let baseball interfere with more important things; he was a tender family man who couldn't wait for each season to end so he could return to his home and family near Frederick, Maryland.

Born September 12, 1916, in Middletown, Maryland, Keller grew up on a dairy farm and attributed his strength to "milking cows when I was a kid, I guess." He hit around .500 in back-to-back seasons at the University of Maryland; at dawn one summer morning in 1936, he was awakened by Yankee scouts Paul Krichell and Gene McCann, who got his signature on a Yankee contract.

Keller joined the Newark Bears the next spring and drew instant comparisons with Babe Ruth. In his first two years of pro ball, Keller won consecutive batting titles in the tough International League, with averages of .353 and .365. He was touted as the greatest prospect ever to come through the Yankee organization.

Some feel Keller never fulfilled his tremendous promise. One reason Charlie's .286 major league average is not higher is that the Yankees ordered a change in his batting style. A left-handed hitter, Keller had hit with power to all fields at Newark. But the Yankees wanted him to pull the ball into the short right-field porch at Yankee Stadium. Charlie dutifully became a pull hitter, hitting more home runs and driving in runs. But there were those who felt Keller was unwisely remade.

Charlie had a sensational rookie year in 1939, hitting .334—one of the highest rookie averages in American League history. In the four-game sweep of Cincinnati in the World Series, he hit .438 with five extra-base hits. He became the first rookie to hit two homers in one World Series game and he supplied the coup de grace when he barreled over catcher Ernie Lombardi. "Break up the Yankees, hell!" one Reds' fan exclaimed. "I'll be satisfied if they'll just break up Keller."

He was a fine outfielder, but it was as a slugger that Charlie made his reputation. He had three 30-homer seasons, three 100-RBI seasons, and five 100-walk seasons. His .518 Yankee slugging average

CHARLIE KELLER (NY Yankees)

has been exceeded only by Babe Ruth, Lou Gehrig, Joe DiMaggio, Mickey Mantle, and Reggie Jackson.

Circumstances often worked against Keller. Three weeks before the 1941 World Series, Keller, who was leading the league in RBIs, 122 to Joe DiMaggio's 112, chipped a bone in his ankle and missed the rest of the season. DiMaggio won the RBI title with 125. But Charlie had his cast removed and hit .389 in the World Series.

After serving in the Merchant Marines in 1944, Keller returned to the Yankees during the 1945 campaign and hit .301 in 44 games. He was New York's top player in 1946, leading the club in most offensive categories, including home runs (30) and RBIs (101). He was leading the league early in June of 1947 in home runs (13) and RBIs (36) when he hurt his back and was lost for the year. Six weeks after he played his final full game, Charlie was still third in the league in home runs.

Keller's mobility was greatly restricted after major back surgery. He was a part-time outfielder and pinch-hitter in 1948 and 1949. He became the third American Leaguer in history to homer in consecutive pinch-hit at bats in 1948.

The Yankees released Keller in December of 1949 and he signed with his old buddy, Tiger Manager Red Rolfe. Said Rolfe, "I don't know whether or not he can play ball. But I got him because he'll lend a touch of class to my team." Keller returned to the Yankees for two games in 1952 and five years later was a Yankee coach.

All-Star

Charlie Keller was an All-Star in 1940, 1941, 1943, 1946, and 1947, but injuries forced him off the roster in 1943 and 1947. As a right fielder in the 1940 game, Keller set a record by making four putouts. He was an unsuccessful pinch-hitter in the 1941 game. But Charlie got the Americans off to a fast start in the 1946 game at Fenway Park by blasting a first-inning two-run homer off Claude Passeau. The Americans won, 12–0, and Keller scored two runs.

Yankee Stats

	G	AB	R	H	2B	3B	HR	RBI	BA
11 Years	1,066	3,677	712	1,053	163	69	184	723	.286
4 World Series	19	72	18	22	3	2	5	18	.306
All-Star Games	3	7	2	1	0	0	1	2	.143

TONY KUBEK

Career

Casey Stengel once said of Tony Kubek, "Who could be more valuable in 50 years of my life?" Signed by the Yankees as a 17-year-old in 1953, Kubek was great in the low minors in 1954 and 1955. Moving up to Denver, he hit .331 in 1956, playing for Manager Ralph Houk as an All-Star shortstop and teaming with Bobby Richardson to form a great double-play combination.

Stengel, who had known Tony's dad as a minor league star (Tony Sr. once hit .350 for the old Milwaukee Brewers), took an interest in Tony in the spring of 1957. Stengel liked Kubek's versatility and the kid made the club, although he wouldn't be 21 until after the World Series. As the league's 1957 Rookie of the Year, Kubek was a swingman, playing 50 games in the outfield, 41 at shortstop, and 38 at third base, handling the burden with a maturity that belied his years. And he hit .297. Then Tony became the second rookie to blast two homers in one World Series game, and he did it in the first World Series game ever played in his hometown of Milwaukee.

Kubek became the Yanks' regular shortstop in 1958, although he would continue to play other positions when needed. He held the shortstop's job through 1965.

Tony missed the first four months of the 1962 season while in the army, but in his first at bat upon returning he blasted a three-run homer. Back at shortstop, Tony hit a career high .314 in 45 games. At 6'3", Kubek looked awkward at shortstop, but he was not. He was never smooth, but he was rangy and was one of the better fielding shortstops in the game. The double-play combination of Kubek and his buddy Bobby Richardson was on a par with Chicago's Luis Aparicio/Nellie Fox combo as the best in the league. Unfortunately, Kubek is remembered best for a play in Game 7 of the 1960 World Series. In the Pirates' comeback rally, Bill Virdon hit a tailor-made double-play grounder that hopped crazily on a rough Forbes Field infield and struck Tony in the throat. All hands were safe, Kubek had to be hospitalized, and the Pirates went on to win.

Kubek was a left-handed contact hitter who sprayed line drives to all fields. He often batted first or second under Manager Houk and hit as many as 14 homers in 1961, the year he set the club record for shortstops with 38 doubles. In a Fourth of July doubleheader against Washington in 1959, Kubek made eight hits in 10 trips.

TONY KUBEK (NY Yankees)

A quiet young man of wholesome tastes, Kubek wore his blond hair short, read self-improvement books, and avoided publicity. He protected his privacy and it wasn't hard for him to fade into the background with so many famous players sharing the same locker room. It is ironic that Kubek would become one of the game's great broadcasters and, in the years that followed, the most visible of the Yanks of his time.

Kubek was plagued by back and neck troubles in his last few years. After a .218 season in 1965, Tony was warned against playing further by doctors concerned about permanent damage. So Kubek intelligently retired at the age of 29.

All-Star
Tony Kubek was on the American League's All-Star team in 1958, 1959, and 1961 and played in the latter two years. He pinch-hit, walked, scored a run, and played left field as the Americans won, 5–3, in the second game of 1959, and he was a starter in the first game of 1961, going hitless in four trips.

Yankee Stats
	G	AB	R	H	2B	3B	HR	RBI	BA
9 Years	1,092	4,167	522	1,109	178	30	57	373	.266
6 World Series	37	146	16	35	2	0	2	10	.240
All-Star Games	2	5	1	0	0	0	0	0	.000

JOHNNY KUCKS

Career

The seventh game of a World Series is not a bad time to pitch your greatest game, which is what Johnny Kucks did. But coming as it did two days after Don Larsen's perfect game in the 1956 World Series, Kucks' clinching three-hitter, masterful as it was, lacked the glimmer of Larsen's perfection. Kucks permitted only one baserunner to reach second, his sinkerball inducing 16 groundball outs. He beat Brooklyn, 9–0.

Born July 27, 1933, in Hoboken, New Jersey, Kucks grew to 6'3". He broke into the Yankee organization with a splendid 19–6 record at Norfolk in 1952, and after two years in the military, made the Yankees in the spring of 1955, going 8–7 his rookie year.

He enjoyed his finest season in 1956. With his sinker dipping nicely, the 23-year-old went 18–9, winning one-third of his 54 lifetime victories. He beat the second-place Indians four times and was second on the New York staff in wins (behind Whitey Ford). Kucks led the club with 31 starts. Johnny made everyone happy with his wins and pleased his fielders in particular with his fast work on the mound.

The big right-hander slipped to 8–10 and 8–8 in the next two seasons and was traded to the Kansas City A's in May of 1959. Johnny was 4–10 for Kansas City in 1960, his last season in the majors.

All-Star

Johnny Kucks was selected to the American League's pitching staff for the 1956 All-Star Game but did not appear in the game played at Washington's Griffith Stadium and won by the Nationals, 7–3.

Yankee Stats

	W	L	PCT	G	GS	CG	SA	SO	ERA
5 Years	42	35	.545	143	83	23	6	249	3.82
4 World Series	1	0	1.000	8	1	1	0	4	1.89
All-Star Games (no appearances)									

JOHNNY KUCKS (Bob Olen)

TONY LAZZERI

Career

Tony Lazzeri is unfairly remembered as the fellow Ronald Reagan . . .
no, Grover Cleveland Alexander, struck out with the bases loaded in
the seventh game of the 1926 World Series to preserve a slim lead for
the Cardinals, who went on to defeat the Yanks. Just before striking
out, Lazzeri lined a ball into the left-field seats that was barely foul.
"Less than a foot made the difference between a hero and a bum,"
Alexander would say. But Tony Lazzeri was one of baseball's greatest
all-round second basemen.

Born on December 6, 1903, Lazzeri grew up in the Telegraph Hill
section of San Francisco. He played shortstop at Salt Lake City in
1925, hitting 60 home runs with 222 RBIs in the 200-game Pacific
Coast League schedule. But the Cubs, who had a working agreement
with Salt Lake City, were not inclined to become very interested: Tony
Lazzeri was an epileptic. But the Yankees took notice and had scouts
Ed Holly and Paul Krichell look him over. The scouts said he was great
and General Manager Ed Barrow purchased Lazzeri's contract for
$50,000 (and several players). Years later, Lazzeri's Salt Lake City
manager, Oscar Vitt, said, "Lazzeri was my baby. He was the greatest
ballplayer I ever handled . . . " Lazzeri experienced one seizure in the
clubhouse but none on the field as a Yankee.

The Yankees needed a second baseman badly when Lazzeri
joined them in 1926, and Yankee Manager Miller Huggins, a former
second baseman, helped Tony make the switch to second. Lazzeri
was teamed with shortstop Mark Koenig and, although they made a
few errors, the new middle infielders were instrumental in leading the
Yankees from next-to-last place the previous season to first place in
1926. Lazzeri knocked in 114 runs and, even though a rookie, was the
leader of the infield, guiding young Lou Gehrig on his left and Koenig
on his right.

Lazzeri was the Yanks' regular second sacker for 12 seasons
(1926–37), although he also played in 267 Yankee games on the left
side of the infield. Making rapid improvement following his jittery
rookie season when he was just one shy of leading the league in
errors, in 1927 Lazzeri fielded .971, just one point below the league
leader. He then maintained his solid fielding through the years.

Lazzeri starred as the best right-handed power hitter in Murderers'
Row. His 18 homers in 1926 were 10 more than the combined total of

TONY LAZZERI (NY Yankees)

all the other regular second basemen in the American League. Tony had four 18-homer years and seven seasons of 100-plus RBIs. He ranks seventh on New York's all-time RBI list. He topped .300 five times, with a high of .354 in 1929.

Lazzeri's greatest game—and he had several—came on May 24, 1936, when he hit a triple, a solo homer, and a pair of grand slams. He is the first player in big league history to hit two grand slams in one game and his 11 RBIs in that game set a league record that still survives.

"Poosh 'Em Up Tony," the first superstar of Italian descent, enjoyed great popularity in Italian circles. The sportswriters, however, were wary of Tony's temper and sullenness. But the players saw a team-mate who mixed in easily with clubhouse banter and who, as a responsible team leader, took youngsters Frank Crosetti and Joe DiMaggio under his protective wing. Quiet Tony had tremendous baseball instincts—he worked the double steal to perfection—and kept his nose hard as well as clean. He played the 1928 World Series with a shoulder so lame he was unable to throw overhand.

Coming off a .244 season in 1937, Lazzeri hit .400 to lead all batters in the World Series. The Yankees then released Lazzeri to the Cubs, opening up second base for young Joe Gordon. Lazzeri helped the Cubs win the 1938 pennant, played for both the Dodgers and Giants in 1939, and ended his great 14-year career with a .292 lifetime average.

All-Star
Tony Lazzeri was selected for the first All-Star Game in 1933, the year after his last .300 season, but he didn't get to play. American Manager Connie Mack stayed with Detroit's Charlie Gehringer at second base for the entire game.

Yankee Stats

	G	AB	R	H	2B	3B	HR	RBI	BA
12 Years	1,658	6,094	952	1,784	327	115	169	1,154	.293
6 World Series	30	105	16	28	3	1	4	19	.267
All Star Games (no appearances)									

JOHNNY LINDELL

Career

In 1941, Johnny Lindell was a 20-game winner at the highest minor league level; three years later, in 1944, he was a 100-RBI man in the majors.

The 18-year-old native of Greeley, Colorado, signed with the Yankees in 1936 for, as Lindell has said, "a handshake, a comb, and a bar of Lifebuoy." Five years later, the rawboned 6'4", 217-pounder, who threw and batted right-handed, won 23 games at Newark and was the Minor League Player of the Year. The next year, 1942, he worked out of the Yankee bullpen, going 2–1 in 23 games.

The Yankees were missing serviceman Joe DiMaggio when the 1943 spring camp opened at Asbury Park, New Jersey, and Manager Joe McCarthy, impressed by Lindell's solid hitting, switched strong-armed Johnny to center field. For two seasons, Lindell roamed the hallowed ground in center.

Lindell, who led the league in triples in both 1943 and 1944, enjoyed his best year in 1944, hitting .300 with 18 homers and 103 RBIs. He entered military service during the 1945 season.

After almost trading Lindell in 1947, the Yankees used him in June to fill the hole left by a fallen Charlie Keller. Johnny stepped in, did an excellent job in left field the rest of the season while knocking in 67 runs, then he hit .500 in the World Series with Brooklyn. Johnny followed 1947 with a .317 season in 1948.

Johnny, whose contract was sold to the Cardinals in 1950, was a happy-go-lucky guy off the field. His teammates loved his coarse, irreverent locker-room humor. But on the field he never let up, hustling as though each game was the seventh game of the World Series. He was so aggressive at spilling pivotmen at second base that a rule was passed to protect them. He was a rabid bench jockey when he rode the pines, and a clutch performer when he played. He was instrumental in winning some big games. He beat Boston with a homer on the next-to-last day of the 1949 season, putting the Yankees into a first-place tie. The next day, New York beat Boston again and won the pennant.

All-Star

Johnny Lindell was an All-Star in 1943 but he didn't see any action in the game won by the Americans, 5–3, at Philadelphia's Shibe Park.

Yankee Stats

	G	AB	R	H	2B	3B	HR	RBI	BA
10 Years	742	2,568	371	707	112	45	63	369	.275
3 World Series	12	34	4	11	3	1	0	7	.324

All-Star Games (no appearances)

JOHNNY LINDELL (NY Yankees)

EDDIE LOPAT

Career

Born June 21, 1918, in New York City, Edmund Walter Lopatynski (or Eddie Lopat) hoped to play first base for the Yankees. But it seemed that Lou Gehrig would have that job forever, and so Eddie began in the minors as a pitcher. That was 1937, and seven years later Eddie moved up to the White Sox. Yankee General Manager George Weiss, in his first big deal, acquired Eddie in February of 1948.

Eddie was Steady Eddie, the Junk Man, the "cute little left-hander." He was the most exasperating pitcher in the majors to bat against. Free swingers especially were baffled by his assortment of slow pitches, all thrown (rather, pitched—Eddie was not a thrower) with pinpoint control. He mixed tantalizing curveballs and screwballs with sliders and a sneaky fastball. All were thrown at different speeds, but with the same motion, and hitters never found their stride. Lopat pulled the string, set hitters up, and outsmarted them. He even got Ted Williams out once on a blooper pitch.

Among former pitchers with at least 100 Yankee decisions, Lopat ranks sixth with a .657 winning percentage. He averaged 16 wins per season over the five consecutive World Championship years (1949–53) and he didn't have a losing season as a Yankee until his eighth and last season. In fact, in each of his first seven Yankee campaigns, Eddie's winning percentage was at least .600. His best season was 1951, when he won 21 games and added two complete-game victories over the Giants in the World Series. Lopat won the ERA title in 1953 (2.42).

The Cleveland Indians finished second behind the Yankees in 1951, 1952, 1953, and 1955; their inability to beat Steady Eddie was one reason for their frequent bridesmaid's role. The Indian killer was 40–12 against Cleveland, including 11 consecutive wins. Lopat once arrived early at Cleveland's Municipal Stadium and, sitting unnoticed in the stands, watched as the Indians practiced hitting against an Eddie Lopat clone who served slow, southpaw curves. The hitters choked up and hit flatfooted the opposite way. Ed smiled at the thought of what lay ahead. That evening, the first time through the Indian order, Lopat threw nothing but jamming fastballs and hard sliders, sawing off Indian bats as the hitters tried to shoot the ball the other way. When the bewildered Indians adjusted to their free-swinging ways, Eddie returned to his off-speed pitches. It was another win for Lopat.

Lopat was waived to Baltimore in the summer of 1955, his final major league campaign. He remained in baseball as a coach, manager, general manager, and scout. He was the Yanks' pitching coach in 1960.

All-Star

Eddie Lopat was an All-Star for the 1951 game played at Detroit's Briggs Stadium. He entered the 1–1 game in the fourth inning and allowed a solo home run by Stan Musial and a two-run shot by Bob Elliott. Ed took the loss as the Nationals won, 8–3.

Yankee Stats

	W	L	PCT	G	GS	CG	SA	SO	ERA
8 Years	113	59	.657	217	202	91	2	502	3.21
5 World Series	4	1	.800	7	7	3	0	19	2.60
All-Star Games	0	1	.000	1	0	0	0	0	27.00

EDDIE LOPAT (NY Yankees)

SPARKY LYLE

Career

He was the Count. Distinguished by a long, curving mustache and a confident strut to the pitcher's mound, Sparky Lyle was a man in control—always of himself and usually of the situation. But Sparky was not a nobleman from a faraway place; he came from the same western Pennsylvania coal country that gave the Yankees another great relief pitcher, Joe Page.

Born July 22, 1944, in DuBois (he grew up in nearby Reynoldsville), Sparky developed into a strong-throwing left-hander. In one 17-inning sandlot game, he used his blazing fastball to strike out 31 batters. This kind of pitching attracted some attention and, in 1964, Sparky signed a pro contract with the Orioles, but was drafted away from the Baltimore organization by Boston.

Sparky began developing his slider while relief pitching in the minors. He broke in with the Bosox in 1967 and over five seasons saved 69 games. The Yankees picked him up in March of 1972 in a bargain deal (for Danny Cater and Mario Guerrero) and suddenly Manager Ralph Houk had himself a bullpen.

The Yankee bullpen in 1971 saved all of 12 games. In 1972, Lyle alone had 35 saves, setting a since-broken league record and a still-standing club high. The league's Fireman of the Year frequently saved both ends of a doubleheader and, in the ninth inning of a game with Texas, he struck out the side on 10 pitches with the bases loaded. His slider was now perfected and he threw little else.

Lyle led the Yankee bullpen six consecutive years (1972–77) in relief points (wins plus saves). Over the 1972–73 seasons, he won or saved 76 of the Yankees' 159 victories. He had only 15 saves in 1974 but sported an ERA of 1.66. After only six saves in 1975, he rebounded with a league-leading 23 saves in 1976 and, having pitched in 66 games in 1974 to set a club record, he broke that record in 1977 by appearing in 72 games. He went 13–5 with 26 saves in 1977 to become the first relief pitcher in American League history to capture the Cy Young Award.

Twice he won three consecutive Yankee games in 1977, once in the dog days of late August and again in the postseason when he won the final two games of the playoffs and the first game of the World Series. Over the latter three games, played under intense pressure, Lyle didn't allow a single run over 10 1/3 innings.

SPARKY LYLE (NY Yankees)

The Count was good under pressure and Yankee fans loved him for it. Armed with one pitch—the darting, elusive slider—he never wilted. One of the game's free spirits—he often sat naked on birthday cakes and during a clubhouse meeting he once emerged from a coffin—Sparky was the life of the party, which he seemed to take to the bullpen where he would munch on cheeseburgers or pastrami sandwiches and talk with friends around the country over the wall phone while waiting for his call to mound duty.

But life in Yankeeland went sour for Sparky late in 1977 when the club signed Rich Gossage. He knew there wouldn't be enough short work for both relievers, one of whom he considered grossly underpaid. His fears came to pass in 1978 when he found himself more and more in long relief while Gossage got the saves. Said teammate Graig Nettles: "In one year Sparky Lyle has gone from Cy Young to sayonara." Lyle went to Texas after the 1978 season in the acquisition of Dave Righetti, then bounced around in baseball for several years. He remains No. 1 on New York's all-time list for saves.

All-Star

Sparky Lyle was an All-Star three times. He was passed over in 1972, his greatest season, American League Manager Earl Weaver believing the skills of a relief pitcher were "too specialized." Lyle pitched one shutout inning in the 1973 game and struck out Willie Mays on three pitches in Mays' last All-Star appearance. Asked afterwards if he felt badly about fanning the legendary Mays, Lyle replied, "Hell, no. Why should I feel bad?"Sparky didn't pitch in the 1976 game, and in the 1977 game at Yankee Stadium he was tagged for two runs in two innings.

Yankee Stats

	W	L	PCT	G	GS	CG	SA	SO	ERA
7 Years	57	40	.588	420	0	0	141	454	2.41
3 Champ. Series	2	0	1.000	6	0	0	1	3	2.31
2 World Series	1	0	1.000	4	0	0	0	5	1.27
All-Star Games	0	0	.000	2	0	0	0	2	6.00

GIL McDOUGALD

Career

The versatility of Gil McDougald, the most deployable infielder in Yankee history, made him the most valuable infielder of the Casey Stengel regime. McDougald, who always held a regular job over his 10-year career (1951–60), played 599 games at second base, 508 at third, and 284 at shortstop. His versatility gave Stengel wide juggling opportunities with his infield, and Stengel made the most of them. Not only could Gil play the positions, but he was the best in the league wherever he played. Three times he led the league in turning double plays—and at three different positions!

McDougald, a San Franciscan, attended City College of San Francisco and broke into the Yankee organization as a 20-year-old in 1948, hitting .340 and .344 in his first two minor league seasons. As Beaumont Manager Rogers Hornsby's second baseman in 1950, McDougald hit .336 and was named MVP of the Texas League.

He impressed Stengel in the 1951 rookie camp, stayed for spring training, made the team, and won Rookie of the Year honors. When Stengel asked him to play third, McDougald accepted the challenge even though he hadn't played the position before. He was moved back to second in mid-season, however. Gil tied a league record, collecting six RBIs in one inning with a two-run triple and a grand-slam homer against St. Louis on May 3. He finished at .306, the club's highest average. And he hit the first grand slam by a rookie in World Series play. Quite a first year!

In each of his first eight seasons, McDougald hit between 10 and 14 home runs. He had an unorthodox right-handed stance that Stengel finally nixed in 1955. The next year, Gil sent stinging line drives to all fields, batted a career high .311, and ran second to Mantle in the MVP voting. But on May 7, 1957, McDougald lined a ball off the face of Cleveland pitcher Herb Score, breaking three facial bones. Score was never the same pitcher and McDougald was never as aggressive as a hitter.

Second-half back spasms in 1958 brought McDougald's average down to .250, his career low. But then he hit .321 in the World Series against Milwaukee and delivered key hits in the fifth and sixth games, helping New York overcome a three-games-to-one deficit.

On the field, McDougald, sometimes called "Smash," was a great competitor and a fearless performer who played better when angry.

GIL McDOUGALD (NY Yankees)

He may have been the third most valuable player in the league behind Mantle and Yogi Berra. Off the field, he was a class act. He was presented the Lou Gehrig Memorial Award in 1958 in recognition of his Gehrig-like qualities. He always had time for autograph seekers.

McDougald had predetermined that 1960 would be his last season. After a season which included a .450 (9-for-20) pinch-hitting mark, McDougald retired while on top, turning aside a lucrative offer to play for the expansion Los Angeles Angels. In 10 years, he had played on eight pennant winners and in 53 World Series games, the fourth most in history.

All-Star
Gil McDougald was a five-time All-Star and was named to the team as a third baseman, shortstop, and second baseman (but he played only at shortstop). He played sparingly in 1952 and 1957, and didn't play in 1956. But in the 1958 game, in Baltimore, he drove in Frank Malzone with the winning run on a sixth-inning pinch single as the Americans won, 4–3. Gil was a pinch-runner for Ted Williams and played shortstop in the first game of 1959.

Yankee Stats

	G	AB	R	H	2B	3B	HR	RBI	BA
10 Years	1,336	4,676	697	1,291	187	51	112	576	.276
8 World Series	53	190	23	45	4	1	7	24	.237
All-Star Games	4	4	1	1	0	0	0	1	.250

GEORGE McQUINN

Career

What happened to George McQuinn 17 years after signing with the Yankees? He made the team. And George McQuinn was a fine, fine ballplayer. The native of Arlington, Virginia, signed by Yankee scout Gene McCann, started in the minors in 1930. He played first base in Wheeling, Scranton, Albany, Binghamton (where he hit .357 in 1933 and was a batting champ), and Toronto.

After a brief and unsuccessful trial with Cincinnati in 1936, McQuinn was returned to the Yankee organization, and in 1937 he hit .330 at Newark. But there was nowhere to go; Lou Gehrig was still playing a strong first base in New York. McQuinn escaped from the logjam by going to the St. Louis Browns.

In St. Louis he had eight solid seasons, beginning with a .324 average and 34-game hitting streak in 1938. Although he was a bag of bones, George was agile and a dancing dandy around first base. He was a big league star finally, but he longed for Yankee pinstripes.

George played for the Philadelphia A's in 1946, hit .225, and was released by Connie Mack. "I'm sorry to lose George," Mack said, "but I really believe he has played baseball one year too long." George called Bucky Harris and was assured of a spring trial with the Yankees. Larry MacPhail, meanwhile, searched for a first baseman (the club's weak link) and rumors were afoot that either Hank Greenberg or Mickey Vernon would come to New York. Neither came and McQuinn, surprising everyone, won the first base job. He got off to a torrid start and was hitting around .390 in late May. He was holding steady at .328 at the All-Star Break and finished at .304. He scored 84 times and knocked in 80 runs. And he was the best Yankee fielder at the bag since the slick Hal Chase. His comeback was the talk of baseball.

A painful back condition finally slowed McQuinn down in 1948. He hit .248 in 94 games and retired at the age of 39. He had performed well for 12 seasons in the majors, finishing with a .276 lifetime average. And he had that one great year on a Yankee World Championship club.

All-Star

As a Brown, George McQuinn played in the 1944 All-Star Game, and he was an American League starter in both his Yankee seasons. He was 0-for-4 in the 1947 game. But in the 1948 game, which the Americans won, 5–2, at Sportsmans Park in St. Louis, George had two hits, scored a run, stole a base, and set a record for putouts by a first baseman with 14.

Yankee Stats

	G	AB	R	H	2B	3B	HR	RBI	BA
2 Years	238	819	117	232	35	7	24	121	.283
1 World Series	7	23	3	3	0	0	0	1	.130
All-Star Games	2	8	1	2	0	0	0	0	.250

GEORGE McQUINN

MICKEY MANTLE

Career

Mutt Mantle was good at baseball. His reputation didn't extend to New York City, but around Commerce, Oklahoma, he was considered an outstanding semi-pro. He loved baseball. He named his first son, born October 20, 1931, after catcher Mickey Cochrane. Mickey Mantle, in Mutt's dreams, would become a major leaguer. Mutt made a switch-hitter out of him..

Mutt Mantle didn't live to see his son reach full flower, but he did have the thrill of seeing him reach the majors. Mickey eventually hit 536 home runs, 373 left-handed and 163 right-handed, easily reaching the Baseball Hall of Fame as a superstar and the greatest switch-hitter the game ever saw.

Mickey was a rawboned youngster playing for the semi-pro Baxter Springs Whiz Kids when he caught the attention of Yankee scout Tom Greenwade, who was later to say, "When I first saw him, I knew how Paul Krichell must have felt the first time that he saw Lou Gehrig." He was signed up for a $1,100 bonus after his graduation from high school and was assigned to the minors where in 1949–50 he hit .313 at Independence and .383 at Joplin.

He was the Yankees' teenage phenom in the spring of 1951, the year the Yanks trained in the West, hitting balls all over the Arizona landscape and all along a tour of the West Coast. Manager Casey Stengel relished having Mickey at the plate but not at shortstop. The Mick did not play the position well, so Stengel moved his 19-year-old slugger to right field, where Mickey opened the season. Mickey's rookie year had its rough spots. He was sent down to the minors but then was brought back to finish with 13 Yankee homers, 65 RBIs, and a .267 average.

Mickey became New York's center fielder for 1952 after Joe DiMaggio retired. He had a strong arm and his burning speed allowed him to cover the big-bellied middle of the Yankee Stadium outfield. He would make tremendous running catches, his most famous catch robbing Gil Hodges and saving Don Larsen's perfect game in the 1956 World Series. Sure-handed, he made only two errors in 1955 and again only two in 1959 to lead the league's outfielders in fielding both years. He played errorless ball in 97 outfield games in 1966.

MICKEY MANTLE (NY Yankees)

Mantle's every swing was exciting. He was a solidly built 200-pounder but he wasn't a giant in the mold of, say, Frank Howard. Yet he consistently hit the ball farther than any player in history. His tape-measure shots include a 565-footer at Washington in 1953 and two shots off the right-field facade at the Stadium, both of them barely staying in the Stadium. The second blast, hit in a 1963 game, may have been the hardest ball ever hit. Scientists said it would have traveled at least 620 feet if the facade of the "old" Stadium's roof hadn't been in the way.

Mantle was the fastest player in the game before he was slowed by injuries. He could reach first base in 3.1 seconds and he resurrected the art of drag bunting. "Nobody was a better drag bunter," Phil Rizzuto said recently in *Sport* magazine. "He used to be so fast that he could just outrun the ball."

But it was the power game that distinguished the Mick's career, right up to the end. He led the league in home runs four times. He hit two homers in a game 46 times. He hit homers from both sides of the plate in the same game a record 10 times. He hit 266 homers at the Stadium, more than anyone else. He hit a record 18 World Series homers, including a grand slam in the 1953 Series. His 536 career homers put him sixth on the all-time list.

Pitchers treated Mantle with respect. Only Babe Ruth, Ted Williams, and Carl Yastrzemski have been walked more often. Mickey led the Yankees in walks 14 times. With 146 walks and 173 hits in 1957, the Mick was on base well over 50 percent of the times he batted. Great on-base percentages like that meant he was in position to score often, and he did. He scored more than 100 runs in nine straight seasons (1953–61), leading the league six of those years.

Mantle fans are galled that he finished under .300 lifetime when he hit better than .300 in 10 of his first 14 seasons, with a high of .365 in 1957. His career average was .309 through 1964, but over his final four years, when he was nearly crippled, he hit a combined .254 to finish at .298 lifetime. To reduce the pounding on his aching legs, he played the 1967–68 seasons at first base.

Mantle's greatest seasons were 1956 and 1961. He led the league in batting (.353), home runs (52), and RBIs (130) in his Triple Crown 1956 season, and in 1961 had a titanic home-run duel with Roger Maris, the two sluggers chasing Babe Ruth's single-season record. Hampered by late-season injuries and illness, Mickey finished with 54.

It took time for Mantle to win the hearts of Yankee fans, who were not always kind to the shy youngster. Some demanded instant Babe

Ruth. DiMaggio devotees resented him. Even Casey Stengel didn't seem satisfied with Mantle's best. But Ralph Houk, who became Yankee manager in 1961, applauded the Mick and gave him confidence. (Mantle's charm rests, in part, on an absence of ego.) The fans took Houk's lead and conferred a kind of hero status on the Mick. Unfortunately, they made Maris into a villain at the same time.

A good case could be made for any one of a number of today's players (George Brett, Robin Yount, Dave Winfield, and so on) as the best all-round player in the American League. No such debate was possible from 1955 through 1964. Mickey Mantle was the greatest player in the league, period. He was the top drawing card, the three-time MVP, and the team leader of the successful Yankees. A youngster once accused Al Kaline of not being half as good as Mickey Mantle. "Son," replied Kaline, "*nobody* is half as good as Mickey Mantle."

The physical problems that plagued Mantle began in high school when a football injury caused osteomyelitis, a bone disease. Then, in the 1951 World Series, he suffered a knee injury that began a series of injuries involving both knees and a shoulder. He was beset by injuries, and yet it was because of an injury that he had one of his greatest thrills. He had broken a bone in his left foot in June of 1963, and after being out for two months was introduced as a pinch-hitter to the Yankee Stadium crowd. He received an ovation so approving and enthusiastic that he felt goose bumps. Mickey repaid the fans for their generosity, hitting a homer that tied the score in the ninth, allowing the Yanks to win in extra innings.

Mantle had his last truly Mantle-like season in 1964 when he was 32. He remained in the game through 1968 and announced his retirement March 1, 1969; the following June his No. 7 uniform was retired in Yankee Stadium ceremonies. Mickey received the ultimate honor in 1974 with his election to the Hall of Fame in his first year of eligibility. He more than fulfilled Mutt Mantle's dream, and in spite of all of his injuries, played in more Yankee games than anyone in history. He was special—truly remarkable.

All-Star
Mickey Mantle was selected to 20 All-Star teams, making the team every year from 1952 through 1968 except 1966, including the two-game years of 1959, 1960, 1961, and 1962. He played in 16 games, more than anyone in a Yankee uniform. He hit safely in a record seven consecutive games (1954–60), and struck out more often (17 times) than anyone in All-Star history.

The Mick had three fine games in a row. He scored a run and made two hits in the 1954 game. He collected two hits at Milwaukee's County Stadium in 1955, one of them a three-run homer off Robin Roberts that traveled some 430 feet. The next year he hit a Warren Spahn pitch for a homer at Washington's Griffith Stadium. The 1968 game was Mickey's last All-Star appearance and, sensing this, the Houston Astrodome crowd gave him an overwhelming ovation.

Mickey was the honorary captain of the American League team in 1975. This was the first year that honorary captains were used, and Stan Musial captained the Nationals.

Yankee Stats

	G	AB	R	H	2B	3B	HR	RBI	BA
18 Years	2,401	8,102	1,677	2,415	344	72	536	1,509	.298
12 World Series	65	230	42	59	6	2	18	40	.257
All-Star Games	16	43	5	10	0	0	2	4	.233

ROGER MARIS

Career

The final game of the season is nearly half over, the count is 2–0 and Roger Maris waits for the next pitch from Boston's Tracy Stallard. The ball gets too much of the plate and Roger parks it in the lower right-field stands at Yankee Stadium. It is Roger's 61st homer of 1961.

Maris was born September 10, 1934, in Fargo, North Dakota, where he starred as a young athlete, once returning four kickoffs for touchdowns in one high school football game. He broke into the majors in 1957 and showed flashes of brilliance in three years with Cleveland and Kansas City. In December of 1959, George Weiss, in his last big deal as Yankee general manager, obtained Maris from the A's.

The Yankees, who had been unusually mediocre in 1959, won 18 more games in 1960, Maris being the single most important factor in their return to first place. Wasting no time, on Opening Day in Boston, Maris rapped four hits, two of them homers. By July he was out in front of Babe Ruth's 1927 60-homer pace. The Rajah finished with 39, one behind league-leader Mantle, but led the league in slugging (.581) and RBIs (112). He hit .283, his Yankee career high, and won the first of two consecutive MVP Awards.

Maris was more than just a longball hitter. He may have been the greatest fielding right fielder in Yankee history. He specialized in sensational catches at, and sometimes in, the right-field stands at Yankee Stadium. Whenever Mickey Mantle was hurt, Maris would do a commendable job as his center-field replacement. He had good speed, which also helped him on the basepaths, where he was daring and intelligent. And he was a nonstop hustler.

Maris, a strong 200-pounder, had a left-handed pull swing that was tailor-made for Yankee Stadium. He got off to a slow start in 1961, hitting only one homer in April. But then he belted 11 in May and followed that with 15 in June. Then he tapered off, but only slightly— 13 in July, 11 in August, 9 in September and 1 in October (the Stallard homer). He hit 30 homers at the Stadium, tying Lou Gehrig's record, and 31 on the road. Maris also won the 1961 RBI title with 142. But he hit only .269 and for that, in the view of a considerable body of both expert and inexpert opinions, deserved at least house arrest. So great was the pressure from all corners on Roger that by the season's end his hair was falling out in clumps.

ROGER MARIS (Don Rice, Staff Photographer, *NY Herald Tribune*)

If anyone were to break the fondly remembered Ruth's record, the fans wanted it to be Mantle. And the baseball commissioner wanted the dirty business over with in 154 games, the number played in 1927. Purists insisted that baseball's 1961 expansion diluted the pitching talent. (Maris hit only two homers off pitchers new to the league in 1961.) But Roger stoically and heroically prevailed and today his is the universally accepted home-run record.

Roger was hounded in 1962. Untrue, even libelous, stories were written about him and even the home fans made life miserable. Yet he had a great year, hitting 33 homers and enjoying his third 100-RBI season in a row. He saved a 1–0 Yankee win in the seventh game of the World Series by gloving Willie Mays' double in the right-field corner and holding the potential tying run at third base.

Injuries and not the critics brought Roger down. He proved himself as one of the game's greats over the 1960–62 seasons. But then came a series of shattering physical problems that included rectal fissure surgery, a hand fracture, and a nagging leg injury. The Yankees traded him to St. Louis in December of 1966; Roger still wasn't through, helping the Cards win pennants in 1967 and 1968. His power was gone, but his hustle was still there.

All-Star

As a member of the Athletics, Roger Maris played in the second All-Star Game of 1959, and as a Yankee, he played in all six games, 1960–62. He was a combined 0-for-6 in 1960 and 1-for-5 in 1961. In the first game of 1962, Roger drove in a run with a long sacrifice fly that Willie Mays caught up against the right-center-field wall, and in the second 1962 game he had a double and an RBI and scored two runs in the Americans' 9–4 triumph at Wrigley Field.

Yankee Stats

	G	AB	R	H	2B	3B	HR	RBI	BA
7 Years	850	3,007	520	797	110	17	203	548	.265
5 World Series	28	107	18	20	3	0	5	10	.187
All-Star Games	6	17	2	2	1	0	0	2	.118

Career

Alfred Manuel Martin's grandmother called him "bellissimo" ("beauti-ful" in Italian), later shortened to "bellie," and finally converted to Billy. He was a good boy, but Billy, born May 16, 1928, in a tough section of Berkeley, California, was street-wise and tough himself. He hit .450 as a senior at Berkeley High, graduated in 1946, and entered pro ball. His second year as a professional was remarkable. He hit .392 with 174 RBIs in 130 games at Phoenix. In 1948 he moved up to play on the Oakland Oaks under Casey Stengel. Stengel then became the Yankees' manager and Martin rejoined him following the 1949 sea-son.

In 1950, Billy the Kid was the cockiest Yankee rookie since Leo Durocher in 1928. Stengel loved Billy's sassiness. Opening the sea-son in Boston, the Yankees fell behind, 9–0. Stengel inserted Martin, who helped New York score nine runs in the eighth inning and storm to a 15–10 victory, Billy becoming the first player in history to get two hits in one inning in his first major league game. His exceptional start notwithstanding, Billy saw little playing time in his first two Yankee seasons.

Billy became the Yanks' second baseman in 1952. He broke two ankle bones in March, but returned two months later to become a regular, hitting .267 and sparking the team with his spirit. He knocked in the big runs in the pennant clincher and saved the seventh game of the World Series with a lunging catch of Jackie Robinson's tricky infield pop late in the game—the bases were loaded, the Yankees were protecting a two-run lead, and the most likely fielders of the pop made no move on the ball.

He weighed only 165 pounds, but Martin could stroke the ball. He hit 15 homers with 75 RBIs in 1953 in a home ballpark that is brutal on right-handed power hitters. In the 1953 World Series, he hit .500 with 23 total bases and drove home the winning run in the bottom of the ninth in the final game to hand Stengel his fifth consecutive World Championship. He won the Babe Ruth Award as the Series' outstand-ing player.

Stengel was accused of favoritism toward Martin. "If liking a kid who will never let you down in the clutch is favoritism," said Casey, "then I plead guilty." Stengel and Yankee fans were joined in their approval of Martin's combative style and ability to wake up a slum-

BILLY MARTIN (NY Yankees)

bering Yankee team. His scraps with Jimmy Piersall, Clint Courtney, and Tommy Lasorda are legendary. He was a great bench jockey, a team leader, a natural winner, and a player with smarts and heart. A good second baseman, Billy also played well at third and shortstop. He hit .257 over 11 seasons; he was tough in the clutch, hitting .333 in 28 World Series games.

Billy donned the Army olive, missing 1954 and returning to the Yankees late in 1955 in time to furnish the spark necessary to lift the Yankees over Cleveland. He hit .300 and then .320 in the World Series, which Brooklyn won. "We should have won," sobbed Billy. "It isn't right for a man like Casey to lose."

Martin was the regular second baseman in 1956 and had a fine year, hitting over .290 until a September slump reduced him to a final .264. He came through with several key hits in the payback victory over the Dodgers in the 1956 World Series.

The famous Copacabana incident took place in May of 1957, and although Martin was not responsible for the slugging of a member of a bowling group with whom partying Yanks had difficulty, General Manager George Weiss, who never liked Billy, made him the scapegoat. A month later Billy was gone. He remained a player until 1961, bouncing around among several clubs, the fire gone from his game.

The fire returned in 1969 when Billy, who had remained in baseball in various capacities, began his major league managerial career. After managing Minnesota, Detroit, and Texas, he became Yankee manager in August of 1975. He won pennants in 1976 and 1977, resigned, came back, and was fired. After three great years at Oakland, Martin was hired as Yankee manager for his third term on January 11, 1983. A four-time Manager of the Year and a brilliant strategist, Martin's plaque will one day hang alongside Stengel's in the glorious Hall at Cooperstown. As one of the greatest managers in baseball history, Martin deserves that honor.

All-Star

Billy Martin was an All-Star in 1956. The junior loop's starting second baseman was Nellie Fox, but Billy got into the game as a pinch-hitter and grounded out. The Nationals won, 7-3.

Yankee Stats

	G	AB	R	H	2B	3B	HR	RBI	BA
7 Years	527	1,717	220	449	70	18	30	188	.262
5 World Series	28	99	15	33	2	3	5	19	.333
All-Star Games	1	1	0	0	0	0	0	0	.000

JOHNNY MIZE

Career

In 1981, 28 years after he hung up his spikes, Johnny Mize was at last voted into the Baseball Hall of Fame. Big Jawn had the numbers to join the greats. He hit .312, belted 359 home runs, and struck out only 524 times over 15 seasons. His .562 slugging average is the eighth highest in history, and 54 times he finished either first, second, or third in yearly league offensive categories.

Mize was a brilliant student of hitting. He was big and burly and he could put a charge into the ball with his brawn, but he was not just a freewheeling slugger. He had a tremendous batting eye, and he had patience. When he got his pitch, he let loose with a sweet stroke that was both fierce and fluid. He was a skilled, graceful hitter.

Big Jawn was a congenial Georgian, who had a "red melonlike, country-farmer face," according to writer Roger Angell. Mize, born in 1913, was a cousin of the second Mrs. Babe Ruth. He broke in with the Cardinals in 1936 and was traded to the Giants in 1942. In August of 1949, the Yankees purchased Mize's contract from the Giants for $40,000. Mize helped win a couple of 1949 games, then suffered a shoulder injury. But against Brooklyn in the World Series he came through with a key pinch-hit.

Mize played 165 games at first base over 1950–51; afterward, he was used mostly as a pinch-hitter deluxe. In only 274 at bats in 1950, he belted 25 homers and had 72 RBIs on 76 hits. On September 15, 1950, Johnny launched three long homers in Detroit to become the first player to hit a trio of homers in six career games. He hit a combined .292 (38-for-130) as a pinch-hitter over the 1951–53 seasons, leading the league in pinch-hits all three years. He smashed a pinch-hit grand-slam homer in 1952 and batted .400 with three homers in the World Series of that year. In 1953, the Big Cat collected 19 pinch-hits (including five straight) and delivered a game-winning pinch-double to snap a nine-game Yankee losing streak.

In five Yankee seasons, Mize played on five World Series champions (1949–53). His prime years were behind him, but Johnny was still a dangerous hitter. Sportswriter Dan Parker observed:

> Your arm is gone, your legs likewise.
> But not your eyes, Mize, not your eyes.

All-Star

Johnny Mize was a nine-time National League All-Star. As a Yankee in 1953, he was an American League All-Star at the age of 40. He delivered a ninth-inning pinch-hit, but the Nationals won, 5–1, in Cincinnati.

Yankee Stats

	G	AB	R	H	2B	3B	HR	RBI	BA
5 Years	375	870	99	230	39	1	44	179	.264
5 World Series	18	42	5	12	2	0	3	9	.286
All-Star Games	1	1	0	1	0	0	0	0	1.000

JOHNNY MIZE (NY Yankees)

THURMAN MUNSON

Career

Thurman Munson was a great receiver, hitter, and team leader. The nucleus of the Yankee teams of the 1970s, he was the last link in a golden chain of Yankee catchers: Dickey, Berra, Howard, Munson. His illustrious career ended tragically on August 2, 1979, when the plane he piloted crashed, killing him.

One of history's 10 greatest catchers and the best for a decade in the American League, Munson grew up as a gritty, squat athlete in Canton, Ohio, where he captained his high school baseball, football, and basketball teams before going on to Kent State. Yankee scout Harry Hesse watched Munson hit .420 in the Cape Cod summer league (the summer of 1967) and advised the Yanks to keep an eye on him. Scout Gene Woodling watched him hit .413 and garner All-American honors as catcher in his senior year at Kent State and advised the Yankees to "GET HIM." Woodling made Munson New York's top draft pick in June of 1968 and signed him for a bonus of $75,000.

Munson hit .301 at Binghamton in 1968, then landed in the Army and spent 1969 shuttling between New Jersey's Fort Dix, Syracuse (.363 in 28 games), and New York (.256 in 26 games). He began 1970 as the Yanks' regular catcher, a job he held until the day he died, although he suffered through a 1-for-30 slump early in the year. Manager Ralph Houk displayed amazing patience with him and was rewarded when Munson finished at .302 to win Rookie of the Year laurels.

But it was Munson's excellence as a receiver that first built his reputation. He tied Elston Howard's club fielding record for a single season with a 1971 percentage of .998. His only error in 615 chances came in Baltimore, when Andy Etchebarren separated him from both the ball and consciousness. Munson played clean but hard; every gritty ounce of him was in the game (his uniform was always the dirtiest on the field), and as a runner he would later repay catcher Etchebarren with a similar bang-bang play at the plate.

Munson was a tough defensive catcher. He blocked the plate like a bulldog and was skilled at tagging incoming runners. Cat-like, he would pounce on bunts or anything else in his territory. He was an aggressive thrower, picking off runners at all bases with one of the quickest releases ever seen. He had a sound arm and led league catchers in assists three times and double plays twice. And he won three Gold Gloves.

Thurman excelled in the mental aspects of catching, especially in calling a game and in handling a pitching staff. He distracted hitters by jabbering with them. He was the field general from the moment he became a regular. Thurman, who in 1976 became the Yankees' first captain since Lou Gehrig, was the heart of the back-from-the-drought championship teams of 1976–78.

Five times he hit over .300, with a high of .318 in 1975. His lifetime .292 average is outstanding, considering the nicks and bruises a catcher accumulates behind the plate. He had three consecutive seasons (1975–77) of 100-plus RBIs and .300-plus averages, becoming the first American Leaguer since Al Rosen in 1952–54 to do so. The right-handed-hitting Munson had amazing bat control and could pull the long ball or stroke a base hit to the opposite field. He was a smart and aggressive baserunner, who stole 14 bases in 1976, the year he was named MVP, becoming the first Yankee to win both Rookie of the Year and MVP Awards.

For many years, Munson was the league's best clutch hitter. He hit .435 in the 1976 playoffs and .529 in the World Series. His average over 30 lifetime postseason games was .357. Only Pepper Martin (.418) and Lou Brock (.391) have exceeded his .373 World Series mark. He hit safely in 15 of 16 World Series games. When the Yankees needed a key hit, Munson more often than not delivered it.

A fiercely determined athlete, Munson drove himself to the top of baseball. He stayed in the lineup late in his career in spite of serious shoulder and knee problems. He played with pain and he played all-out, enjoying the respect of teammates and opponents alike—he was a player's player. But he was also sensitive about what was said about him. He could be gruff with reporters; the MVP the Baseball Writers awarded him was not won, he conceded, "on popularity." He had a uniquely biting sense of humor, but he was a warm family man, learning aviation so that he could get home faster and more often and thus spend more time with his family.

A Yankee Stadium plaque honors Munson with the words, "Our captain and leader has not left us today, tomorrow, this year, next . . . Our endeavors will reflect our love and admiration for him." His No. 15 uniform has been retired and the Yankee community now awaits the Cooperstown enshrinement of their rugged catcher.

All-Star

Thurman Munson was a seven-time All-Star, making the team in 1971 and 1973–78 (although he was removed from the 1978 roster because of an injury). He was a starter in 1975 and 1976 and appeared in four other games. When injuries prevented Carlton Fisk, the elected starter, from playing in the 1974 game, Thurman stepped in and doubled in three trips and scored a run. But the Nationals won, 7–2, in Pittsburgh.

Yankee Stats

	G	AB	R	H	2B	3B	HR	RBI	BA
1 Years	1,423	5,344	696	1,558	229	32	113	701	.292
3 Champ. Series	14	62	8	21	4	0	2	10	.339
3 World Series	16	67	11	25	5	0	1	12	.373
All-Star Games	6	10	1	2	1	0	0	0	.200

THURMAN MUNSON (NY Yankees)

BOBBY MURCER

Career

On September 14, 1965, fan-favorite Bobby Murcer hit his first major league home run in Washington, D.C. Bobby Richardson was a runner and Lyndon B. Johnson was running the country a few blocks from the Senators' ballpark (then D.C. Stadium, now Robert F. Kennedy Stadium). A lot can change in the course of a baseball career: Richardson has been out of the majors for 17 years, the Johnson presidency ended 14 years ago, and the Senators skipped the nation's capital 12 years ago. Bobby Murcer carries on.

Bobby had just turned 18 when Yankee scout Tom Greenwade signed him for a reported $20,000 bonus in June of 1964. A three-sport high school athlete in Oklahoma City, he hit .458 in his final schoolboy year. As a pro, he hit .365 at Johnson City in 1964 and .322 at Greensboro in 1965, earning an 11-game stint that season with the Yankees; he was only 19, looked younger, and was quiet and a little in awe of his famous Yankee teammates. In 1966 he played 21 games in New York, then spent the rest of the season at Toledo. Army duty cancelled his 1967 and 1968 seasons.

The similarities between Bobby, who returned to the Yankees in the spring of 1969, and Mickey Mantle, who retired at about the same time, were engaging. Both were Oklahomans who were signed by the same scout, and both could give the ball a ride. (Both also began as shortstops and were moved to the outfield.)

Murcer began 1969 playing third base, but he wasn't an infielder. After making three wild throws once, Bobby fielded a grounder and a fan screamed, "Look out, he's got it again!" He was moved to right field and eventually to center field. But Bobby made a remarkably quick transition to major league pitching, hitting 26 homers with 82 RBIs in his first full season.

For a player of relatively slight frame, Murcer generates great power with a "quick bat," and through 1982 has 251 homers and seven 20-plus homer seasons. He was especially productive from 1971 through 1973, hitting a combined .308 with 80 homers and 285 RBIs. Bobby hit a career high .331 in 1971, finishing only six points behind batting champion Tony Oliva. He led the circuit the next year in runs scored (102) and total bases (314).

A Gold Glove winner in 1972, he was an outstanding center fielder, with good instincts, above-average speed, and a good arm. He led

BOBBY MURCER (NY Yankees)

league outfielders in assists three times. So it came as something of a shock when Manager Bill Virdon shifted him to right field in 1974.

Even more of a shock—Murcer was traded to the Giants following the 1974 season. But after several fine years for the Giants and Cubs, Bobby was reacquired by the Yankees in June of 1979. Delighted fans welcomed him back with an overwhelming ovation. Bobby was happy to be reunited with buddy Thurman Munson, but less than two months later, he would give one of the eulogies at Thurman's funeral. That very night, Bobby knocked across all five runs in New York's 5–4 victory over Baltimore in a moving performance at the Stadium.

Murcer has been a part-time designated hitter and pinch-hitter in his second tour with the Yankees. In only 297 at bats in 1980, he has collected 13 homers, 57 RBIs and 13 game-winning RBIs. When the Yankees looked as though they were going to blow a big lead to Baltimore in 1980, Murcer was one of the stout veterans who came through with clutch performances in late August to turn back the threat. He has accepted his role, even thriving on it, which is a mark of a classy old pro. He is relaxed in pressure situations, yet has keen concentration. He has always been a player who plays the game the way it was meant to be played.

All-Star

Bobby Murcer has been a five-time All-Star, four times with the Yankees (1971–74) and once with the Giants (1975). He started in center field in 1971 (replacing the injured Tony Oliva), 1972 and 1974, and started in left field in 1973. He went 1-for-3 in the 1971 game at Tiger Stadium as the Americans won, 6–4, to break an eight-game losing streak.

Yankee Stats

	G	AB	R	H	2B	3B	HR	RBI	BA
12 Years	1,247	4,406	639	1,227	190	29	174	686	.278
2 Champ. Series	2	7	0	1	0	0	0	0	.143
1 World Series	4	3	0	0	0	0	0	0	.000
All-Star Games	4	11	0	1	0	0	0	0	.091

JOHNNY MURPHY

Career

Relief pitcher Johnny Murphy was a trail-blazer. Not that he wasn't preceded by other great relievers (Firpo Marberry of the Senators and Wilcy Moore of the Yankees, to name two), but Johnny was the first to fill the role over a lengthy period. He brought respectability and even glamour to relief pitching, and he was an indispensable member of seven pennant-winning Yankee teams.

Born July 14, 1908, in New York City, Murphy was a hometown star at Fordham Prep and Fordham University. He was signed shortly before his 1929 graduation and began a largely unimpressive career in the minors. He got into two Yankee games in 1932 and was rocked. Newark Manager Al Mamaux put him in the bullpen in 1933 and Murphy's career blossomed; he made 20 consecutive relief appearances during the season without being scored against.

Murphy made the 1934 Yankees and filled in as a starter when injuries hit the pitching staff. Half of his 40 appearances were starts. He won 14 games and had a 3.12 ERA, third best in the league. He was somewhat hesitant when Joe McCarthy asked him in 1935 to become a relief specialist—the bullpen was for over-the-hill starters and kids not yet ready for starting assignments. Murphy reminded McCarthy that relief pitchers drew second-rate salaries; McCarthy assured him that he would receive a starter's pay if he did the job. Years later, Johnny said he enjoyed the role, but only because he was performing it for McCarthy and the Yankees, a man and an organization ahead of the times in the value they put on relief pitching.

Johnny, whom McCarthy called his "pennant insurance," threw just an average fastball. He did have a beautiful curveball and, for that reason, McCarthy liked to use Murphy to induce double-play grounders in tight situations.

Murphy led the league four times in saves and six times in relief wins in the years 1935–43. He led the Yankees in saves 10 times, more often than anyone in club history. Among retired relief pitchers with 200 or more games pitched in relief, Johnny ranks first in the percentage of his games he either won or saved, with 180 wins and saves in 375 relief games—a 48-percent ratio. Lefty Gomez, late in his great career, often entrusted leads to Murphy. When Lefty took a job at a defense plant in 1943, he was asked what it was like. "It's all

JOHNNY MURPHY (Bill Greene, NY World Telegrams)

very strange," he quipped. "I work eight hours a day—and no Murphy to relieve me."

Ten of Murphy's 12 Yankee campaigns were winning seasons. The right-hander was 13–4 in 1937, saved 19 games in 1939, and had a 1.98 ERA in 1941, his best years in each category. He either won or saved a game in six different World Series, with an overall record of 2–0 with four saves. His biggest thrill was saving the final game of the 1936 Series. Johnny relieved Gomez in the seventh inning and, holding the tying run on third, retired the final two Giants. His teammates broke the game open, Johnny recorded the final six outs, and the Yankees were World Champions.

Murphy had a four-pack of nicknames—"Grandma," "Fireman," "Fordham Johnny," and "Rocking Chair Johnny" (the first and last stemming from his rocking delivery). He was a quiet leader, a thoughtful player committed to the team concept. A leader in establishing a players' union in 1946, he was the Yanks' first player representative.

Grandma voluntarily retired in 1944 to take a defense job, but returned to the Yankees in 1946. He was released the following April and went to the Red Sox, with whom he appeared in 32 games before retiring. He remained in baseball and in 1967 became the Mets' general manager. He died of a heart attack shortly after leading the Mets to the miracle World Championship in 1969.

All-Star

Johnny Murphy was uniquely honored for a relief pitcher of his day by his selection to American League All-Star teams in 1937 and 1939. He did not pitch in either game.

Yankee Stats

	W	L	PCT	G	GS	CG	SA	SO	ERA
12 Years	93	53	.637	383	40	17	104	369	3.54
6 World Series	2	0	1.000	8	0	0	4	8	1.10
All-Star Games (no appearances)									

GRAIG NETTLES

Career

When the 1970s began, Brooks Robinson was the American League's best all-round third baseman and Ron Santo the National League's; when the decade closed, George Brett and Mike Schmidt were their respective leagues' top third basemen. But the best over the whole of the 1970s was Graig Nettles. Only Carl Yastrzemski and Reggie Jackson drove in more runs in the American League over the 10 years. And no one—but no one—fielded his position better than did Graig.

The San Diego native, drafted as a 20-year-old by Minnesota in June of 1965, broke into the majors with the Twins in 1967 and reached stardom with the Indians in 1970. The Yankees heisted Nettles from Cleveland for four nonstars in November of 1972; five years later Graig was selected in a poll as the Yankees' All-Time Third Baseman.

Nettles has been one of the finest fielding third basemen in history, ranking right up there with Robinson, Clete Boyer, and Billy Cox. Graig has combined all the requisites—great reflexes, a sure glove, a strong and accurate throwing arm, timing on diving catches, and sharp eyes—with an intelligent handling of his position. He plays deeper and farther off the third base line than other third sackers, allowing him to cover more ground. Yet, because of his quickness, he still guards the line brilliantly. (His only "hole" is a well-placed bunt.) Graig's range cannot be questioned—he has led league third basemen in assists five times.

With Cleveland in 1971, Nettles set major league records for third basemen by making 412 assists and 54 double plays. Two years later he had 410 assists with the Yankees. He set the Yanks record for third basemen with a .975 fielding average in 1978. But it was in the 1978 World Series that Nettles' glovework finally received national attention. He turned the Series around with several miracle plays against the Dodgers in the third game.

Nettles has hit 230 home runs as a Yankee through the 1982 season, placing him sixth on the club's all-time list behind immortals Babe Ruth, Mickey Mantle, Lou Gehrig, Joe DiMaggio, and Yogi Berra. Long known for his streak hitting, Nettles hit 11 homers in April of 1974 to set a league mark and 32 homers in 1976 to lead the league. In 1977, Graig hit 37 homers with 107 RBIs, setting club records for third basemen. His 300 homers as a third baseman is an American League record. No one has hit more homers than Graig's 95 in "new" Yankee Stadium.

GRAIG NETTLES (NY Yankees)

Nettles, a .250 hitter going into the 1983 season, is the kind of player that makes his first hit of the day a 10th-inning game-winning homer. His clutch hitting has been as valuable to the Yankees as his fielding. He was the MVP of the 1981 Championship Series against Oakland, when he hit .500 with a record nine RBIs in a three-game sweep.

But Nettles' game is more than just fielding and hitting. "Having Nettles on your team," Billy Martin once said, "is like having a manager on the field at all times." Nettles may be the smartest and most alert player in the game (he is considered managerial timber), and a leader, becoming the sixth Yankee captain in 1982. Although Graig is not fast, he has been New York's smartest baserunner for years—always alert, daring, taking extra bases, seldom getting caught, making few mistakes. And Graig was durable as a younger player, never playing fewer than 155 games in his first six Yankee seasons.

Nettles' sense of humor rounds out the man. His teammates call him Puff; they'd be talking to him one minute, he'd make a wisecrack, and the next minute be gone, like a puff of smoke. Graig can put crazy circumstances into perspective. "When I was a little boy, I wanted to be a baseball player and join a circus," Graig said during the wacky 1978 season. "With the Yankees, I've accomplished both." As usual, the Yankees welcomed several new faces to spring training in 1983. Or as Graig put it, "Every year, staying here is like getting traded." When you've hit 313 homers with 1,011 RBIs in the majors, you can afford to enjoy yourself.

All-Star

Graig Nettles has been a five-time Yankee All-Star (1975 and 1977–80). He started the 1975 game, played in Milwaukee and won by the Nationals, 6–3, got one hit in four trips and stole a base. Graig also played in 1977 and 1978 and got a hit in 1979. In 1980, George Brett, the league's top vote-getter at third base, was injured and Nettles started the game, going 0-for-2.

Yankee Stats

	G	AB	R	H	2B	3B	HR	RBI	BA
10 Years	1,406	5,057	694	1,273	185	17	230	759	.252
5 Champ. Series	19	70	9	19	3	1	5	17	.271
4 World Series	19	68	4	15	2	0	0	5	.221
All-Star Games	5	9	0	2	0	0	0	0	.222

IRV NOREN

Career

Irv Noren was an outstanding defensive outfielder and a good all-round player, who might have been great had it not been for his failing legs. As it was, he lasted 11 years in the majors and hit a solid .275.

The native of Jamestown, New York, broke into professional baseball in 1946 as a 22-year-old prize prospect of Branch Rickey and the Brooklyn Dodger organization. He won MVPs in the Texas League in 1948 and the Pacific Coast League in 1949. Then his contract was sold to Washington, where he drove in 98 runs as a rookie in 1950.

Noren, a left-handed hitter with little power (65 lifetime homers), became a Yankee because of a problem Yankee Manager Casey Stengel was having in center field early in the 1952 season. Joe DiMaggio had retired and Joe's natural successor, Mickey Mantle, was slow in recovering from a knee injury. So in May, New York traded four players, including Spec Shea and Jackie Jensen, for Noren, who exclaimed upon joining the Yanks, "I just can't believe I'm here!" Noren filled the hole in center field, and when Mantle took over a few weeks later he was moved to left where he was a regular in 1954 and 1955. Noren was a gifted flychaser and a handy, able replacement at first base.

Irv had operations performed on both knees and played with pain throughout his Yankee career. It would take him some time after each game to get his legs straightened out—literally. His ailing legs may have foreclosed on a superstar career, but Irv Noren was a popular member of the Yankee cast. He was a team player, had a good attitude, lived a clean life, and did whatever Stengel asked of him.

His biggest Yankee hit was his score-tying, eighth-inning homer in Philadelphia in a September 26,1952,game that the Yankees went on to win in extra innings to clinch the pennant. In the World Series that followed, Irv hit .300. He led the league in 1954 with a batting average that danced around .350 before a September slump. He finished third at .319, behind Bobby Avila (.341) and Minnie Minoso (.320). Noren, who was traded to the Kansas City A's as part of a blockbuster 13-player deal in February of 1957, had an inside-the-park grand-slam homer in Kansas City in 1955.

All-Star
Irv Noren was on the American League's All-Star team in 1954 when the Americans won, 11–9, in Cleveland. He played in left field but didn't get to hit.

Yankee Stats

	G	AB	R	H	2B	3B	HR	RBI	BA
5 Years	488	1,451	214	394	66	15	31	198	.272
3 World Series	11	27	0	4	0	0	0	2	.148
All-Star Games	1	0	0	0	0	0	0	0	.000

IRV NOREN (NY Yankees)

JOE PAGE

Career

Life was not easy in the nice-sounding western Pennsylvania towns of Cherry Valley and Springdale where Joe Page was born and reared. It became especially tough when the Great Depression settled down upon the coal-mining Pages. Joe, born October 28, 1917, was in his early teens; one day he would use his ability to fire a fastball to escape the hard times of the Allegheny Valley.

Joe was pitching sandlot ball when Yankee scout Bill "Fried" Haddock spotted a potential in him that other scouts failed to see. The southpaw was signed at the age of 23 and sent to Butler, where he fanned 141 in 98 innings.

He joined the Yankees as a starter in 1944 and won five of his first six starts, but then lost six straight games and was sent down to Newark for more seasoning. In the next two years, he pitched for New York but without particular distinction in either starting or relieving roles.

The turning point in his career came on May 26, 1947, when he entered in relief with Boston leading, 3–1. After Ted Williams reached on an error to load the bases, Joe struck out Rudy York and Bobby Doerr, but not before running the count to 3–0 on both batters. Joe got the third out and walked off the field to a standing ovation from a packed house at Yankee Stadium. New York rallied to win, 9–3. Afterwards, Yankee Manager Bucky Harris commented, "If Page had walked York, he was through as a Yankee." But Page was just beginning as the best relief pitcher in baseball, a distinction he would hold for four seasons.

Page finished 1947 as the league leader in both saves (17) and relief wins (14). His contribution to the Yankees' pennant-winning season was singled out by Harris (who was unrestrained in his praise) on the day the Yanks clinched the pennant, and he won the seventh game of the World Series, pitching the final five innings without allowing a run and beating Brooklyn, 5–2. He faced 15 batters and recorded 15 outs.

If Johnny Murphy gave relief pitching respectability, Page gave it status. He could "get the fire out quick," as Stengel said; he was the first reliever to use the strikeout as a prime weapon. Joe was a 6'3" 200-pounder, who threw a rising fastball that had plenty of hop and was especially hard to follow in the late-afternoon shadows at Yankee Stadium. The Stadium fans loved to watch Joe vault over the low right-field bullpen fence, saunter to the mound, scowl toward the plate, and pour fastballs right by hapless hitters. Page saved so many games for Allie Reynolds (as did Murphy for Lefty Gomez) that Reynolds' wins became known as Reynolds-Page victories.

JOE PAGE

A live-for-today Irishman, Page had a reputation for keeping late hours. He enjoyed being a celebrity; he was a friendly fun-lover whose handsome face was always ready with a quick and easy smile. McCarthy couldn't tolerate Page's curfew violations, but his successors, Bucky Harris and Casey Stengel, were more lenient and Page prospered under them. Joe was carefree but not uncaring. His mother, sister, and father all died within a year and Joe looked after several brothers and sisters.

Page reported to camp 30 pounds overweight in 1948, weakened himself through crash dieting, and had an off-year. He rebounded in 1949, leading the league in saves (27) and relief wins (13) and becoming the first reliever to accumulate 40 relief points (saves plus relief wins). On the next-to-last day of the season, Page pitched 6 2/3 scoreless innings against Boston to gain a win, and the next day the Yankees beat Boston to win the pennant. Many considered Page the club's MVP and Connie Mack said he was the greatest reliever he had ever seen. He earned the Babe Ruth Award in the five-game World Series triumph over Brooklyn, winning the third game and saving the fifth.

Fame left Joe Page as quickly as it came. He collected 13 saves in 1950 but had a tired arm, and in the spring camp of 1951, Joe slipped on the mound, threw off balance, and tore a muscle in his pitching arm. He was never the same again, although there was a brief comeback attempt with Pittsburgh in 1954.

All-Star

Joe Page was a three-time All-Star. He was selected for the 1944 game in Pittsburgh. But on the day of his triumphant return to his home area, his father died and Joe did not appear in the game. He earned a save in the 1947 game won by the Americans, 2–1, at Wrigley Field. He entered with two on and two out in the eighth and retired Enos Slaughter, then set down the Nationals in the ninth. Page didn't play in the 1948 game.

Yankee Stats

	W	L	PCT	G	GS	CG	SA	SO	ERA
7 Years	57	49	.538	278	45	14	76	515	3.45
2 World Series	2	1	.667	7	0	0	2	15	3.27
All-Star Games	0	0	.000	1	0	0	1	0	0.00

MONTE PEARSON

Career

The Yankees won four World Championships in Monte Pearson's first four years (1936–39) with the club. Pearson came to New York along with fellow pitcher Steve Sundra in a deal with Cleveland that cost the Yankees gifted pitcher Johnny Allen. Monte went 19–7 in his first year in New York.

Montgomery Marcellus Pearson, a native of Oakland, California, compiled a 36–31 record with Cleveland from 1932 through 1935. The 27-year-old right-hander had a league-leading .731 winning percentage in his first year with the Yanks. Over the next three years, he posted records of 9–3, 16–7, (10 of his wins were consecutive victories in this 1938 season), and 12–5.

Pearson was sensational in October. He won one game in each of the 1936, 1937, 1938, and 1939 World Series, posting a perfect 4–0 record. Overall, Monte allowed only 4.79 hits per nine innings, the second lowest average (behind Jesse Barnes' 4.78) in the history of the Fall Classic. He flirted with a no-hitter in the second game of the 1939 Series, but Cincinnati's Ernie Lombardi singled with one out in the eighth inning to ruin the bid. Pearson settled for a two-hit shutout.

Next to Don Larsen's perfect game, Pearson may have pitched the second greatest game in Yankee Stadium history when, on August 27, 1938, he tossed the first no-hitter in the Stadium's 15-year history. Monte walked two, but he faced the minimum of 27 Indians, the walks eliminated on double plays. Monte had a habit of complaining of a sore arm or illness on his pitching days and was louder than ever in his complaints on this day.

Pearson was only a .228 lifetime hitter, but Monte and Red Ruffing put on a great hitting display on June 17, 1936, when the Yankees swept a doubleheader from Cleveland. Ruffing made four hits in the opener and Pearson added four more in the nightcap. Eight hits on the day from two Yankee pitchers!

After a 7–5 season in 1940, Pearson was dealt to Cincinnati. He went 1–3 in 1941 and finished his major league career with exactly 100 wins.

All-Star

Monte Pearson was a two-time All-Star. He was selected to the American League's All-Star team in 1936 and 1940 but did not play in either game.

Yankee Stats

	W	L	PCT	G	GS	CG	SA	SO	ERA
5 Years	63	27	.700	121	114	54	2	406	3.81
4 World Series	4	0	1.000	4	4	3	0	28	1.01
All-Star Games (no appearances)									

MONTE PEARSON

JOE PEPITONE

Career

Joe Pepitone was one outstanding Yankee of Italian descent whom the club didn't have to go to San Francisco to find; they only needed to look as far as the Park Slope section of Brooklyn. The Yankees signed the Manual Training High School (later renamed John Jay High School) youngster in August of 1958, two months before his 18th birthday, for a $25,000 bonus. Three years later, Pepitone was hitting .316 with 21 home runs at Amarillo.

He split the 1962 season between New York and Richmond. The night in May that Pepitone hit two Yankee homers in one inning helped convince the front office that Joe was their future, and Bill Skowron was traded after the 1962 season.

Replacing the popular Skowron at first base in 1963 might have been a burden for most players, but not for the loose Pepitone. He hit 12 homers in spring training, two on Opening Day, and finished the year with 27 (hitting .271 with 89 RBIs). The following season, Joe had 100 RBIs, including 30 in September in a tough pennant fight. Then he hit a grand slam in the World Series.

Even when Pepitone first came up and was a skinny 6'2", he could sting the ball from his left-handed deep crouch. His quick hands and bat made him a natural pull power hitter at Yankee Stadium, and Joe had four 25-plus home run seasons in seven full Yankee seasons, including 31 in 1966. He hit 219 homers in the majors. His home run ratio of 23.27 ranks just below Stan Musial's 23.10 on the all-time list.

Pepitone was also spectacular with the glove. He was the Yanks' regular first baseman from 1963 through 1969, except for 1967–68 when he played a decent center field. He had good speed for a big man. But he was a wizard at first base, winning Gold Gloves in 1965, 1966, and 1969. He was smooth and graceful around the bag and fielded .997 in 1965 to set a club record.

As immense as his on-the-field ability was, Pepitone's flair always attracted more attention. Indeed, he was one of the most colorful men ever to wear pinstripes. Pepi came to the Yankees with a tough-guy-from-Brooklyn image and left as a longhaired, peace-sign-waving hipster. He drew hip supporters and reactionary antagonists to every ballpark in the league. He was unconventional, daring, distinctive, and individualistic—a man of the changing 1960s. At a time when many players still wore flattops, the longhaired Pepitone brought a hair dryer to the locker room. And no one had more fun than Joe. If he couldn't have fun and play baseball, well, he'd rather not play baseball. A generation of Yankee fans loved him.

The Yankees traded Pepitone to Houston for Curt Blefary in December of 1969. In 1980, Joe rejoined the Yankees as a minor league instructor and in 1982 was a Yankee batting coach.

All-Star

Joe Pepitone was an All-Star in 1963, 1964, and 1965. In his first full big league season, Pepi started the 1963 game and went hitless in four trips as the Nationals won, 5–3, in Cleveland. He was a pinch-runner and defensive replacement in the 1964 game and struck out as a pinch hitter in the 1965 game.

Yankee Stats

	G	AB	R	H	2B	3B	HR	RBI	BA
8 Years	1,051	3,841	435	967	113	24	166	541	.252
2 World Series	11	39	1	6	1	0	1	5	.154
All-Star Games	3	5	0	0	0	0	0	0	.000

JOE PEPITONE (NY Yankees)

FRITZ PETERSON

Career

Fritz Peterson was one of the finest left-handers in Yankee history and one of the game's great control pitchers. He had the misfortune of playing for poor Yankee teams.

Fred Ingels Peterson, a Chicagoan and a graduate of Northern Illinois University, was signed by Yankee scout Lou Maguolo in 1963. Fritz had been an outstanding wing in semi-pro hockey, but now, at 23, began a climb through the Yankee farm system. In 1965, he was 11–1 with Greensboro and 5–5 with Columbus (Georgia); the next spring he made the Yankees.

Peterson had a fine rookie year, tying Mel Stottlemyre for the most Yankee wins with 12. Six of his 11 losses were by one run and two of these were 1–0 defeats. This frustration would be oft-repeated—he was beaten 38 times lifetime by shutout. The Yanks finished last in 1966, the first of eight consecutive seasons in which he was one of the top three starters on the worst Yankee teams since the pre-Ruth era.

In 11 big league seasons, Fritz walked only 426 men in 2,218 innings for a 1.73 walk ratio that is 12th lowest in history. Pinpoint control helped Fritz keep the bases clear; the curveballer allowed only 10.72 baserunners per nine innings, comparable to the great Warren Spahn's 10.75.

Fritz' best season was 1970 when he went 20–11 and walked only 40 men in 260 innings pitched. To win his 20th, he had to journey to Boston and was distressed to find that his hotel room's number was 1219. He asked for a new room, explaining, "If I lose, my record will be 19–12, which is the reverse of 1219." Peterson was lifted from the game and waited nervously in Manager Ralph Houk's office while relief help finished. When the team came in, he asked, "Who won?" Peterson had, and he joined Herb Pennock, Lefty Gomez, Eddie Lopat, and Whitey Ford as the fifth Yankee southpaw to win 20 games.

Fritz was popular with his teammates but was true to the legacy of flaky left-handers. (He would change after baseball, turning to religion.) He was the king of the practical jokers, whether he was ordering magazine subscriptions in Stottlemyre's name or putting a bullfrog into the protective cup pouch of Gene Michael's jockstrap. But it was no practical joke in 1973 when Peterson and teammate

Mike Kekich announced that they had traded families—wives, kids, pets, and all. The following April, Peterson himself was traded to Cleveland. His career ended in 1976 with Fritz' lifetime mark at 133–131.

All-Star
Fritz Peterson was an All-Star in 1970 when the National League won, 5–4, in 12 innings in Cincinnati. He pitched to one batter and allowed a hit in the ninth inning when the Nationals rallied to tie.

Yankee Stats

	W	L	PCT	G	GS	CG	SA	SO	ERA
9 Years	109	106	.507	288	265	81	1	893	3.10
All-Star Games	0	0	.000	1	0	0	0	0	0.00

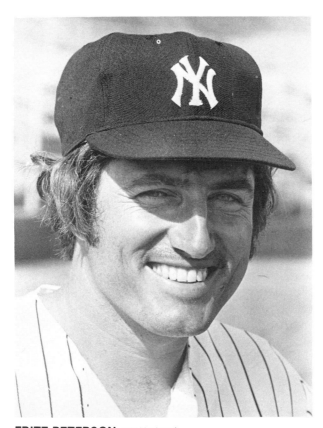

FRITZ PETERSON (NY Yankees)

WILLIE RANDOLPH

Career

Willie Randolph was born July 6, 1954, in Holly Hill, South Carolina. He grew up in Brooklyn's Brownsville section, where he played ball at Tilden High School, and in 1972 was drafted and signed by Pittsburgh. He reached Pittsburgh for 30 late-season games in 1975 and that December was obtained by the Yanks, along with Dock Ellis and Ken Brett, in exchange for Doc Medich.

The pressure was on 21-year-old Randolph at Ft. Lauderdale in the spring of 1976. But Willie had the superior speed and slick glove the scouts had promised and won the second base job. It was no coincidence that the Yankees won their first pennant in 12 years in Randolph's rookie year; he gave them the best second baseman's play since the prime of Bobby Richardson.

Since making the Yanks, Randolph has been ranked along with the Royals' Frank White, who has the advantage of playing on artificial turf, as the best fielding second basemen in the American League. Willie has great range, quick hands and feet, and almost always makes the smart play. He turns the double play beautifully and makes both the spectacular plays and the routine. He teamed for 5 1/2 seasons with shortstop Bucky Dent to form one of the classic double-play combinations. He led the league's second sackers in 1979 in putouts, assists, and double plays.

Willie is a versatile offensive player and a fine leadoff man. He has great speed. He has had four 30-plus stolen-base seasons, and he began the 1983 season sixth on the Yanks' all-time list with 178 stolen bases, only 70 behind Hal Chase, the club's all-time leader. He has skillful bat control and a sharp batting eye—he almost always makes contact. Few players judge balls and strikes better than Willie, who in 1980 walked 119 times, the most ever by a Yankee second baseman. He drew nine walks in the 1981 World Series, breaking Babe Ruth's 1923 record for a six-game Series. With a good stick (and power to right-center field) and a good batting eye, Willie gets on base and scores. He has scored between 85 and 99 runs in each of five seasons.

Like the other holdovers from the Yankees' glory years of the late 1970s, Randolph comes through when the pressure is heaviest. In the 1977 playoffs against Kansas City, it was Willie's sacrifice fly that drove in the winning run in the Yankees' dramatic ninth-inning rally. In

WILLIE RANDOLPH (NY Yankees)

the third game of the 1981 playoffs against Oakland, Willie hit a late-inning homer to break a scoreless tie and spur the Yanks to complete a sweep.

Randolph never had an off-year until the strike-curtailed campaign of 1981, when he hit .232. But in 1982, he finished at .280 (batting over .300 into early June, slumping in mid-summer, and hitting .398 over the final 23 games).

Willie has had leg problems through the years. He has sustained injuries to both knees, and suffered hamstring pulls and groin pulls. The dog days of summer really get him dragging, but he is too valuable to rest very often. He may be the most indispensable everyday Yankee. He leads in a quiet and businesslike fashion. He has handled fame well, living quietly with his family in New Jersey and doing considerable community work.

All-Star

In 1976, Willie Randolph became the first American League rookie to appear on the All-Star ballot since the fans were given back the vote. He made the team but had to bow off the roster because of an injury. He was elected again in 1977, 1980, and 1981.

Randolph started and went all the way in the 1977 game that was played at Yankee Stadium and won by the Nationals, 7–5. He had one hit in five at bats and set a nine-inning All-Star record for second basemen with six assists.

When top vote-getter Paul Molitor was injured in 1980, Willie made the start and cracked two hits. He also got picked off first base and made two errors. He started the 1981 game and went 1-for-3.

Yankee Stats

	G	AB	R	H	2B	3B	HR	RBI	BA
7 Years	934	3,477	578	949	134	48	25	289	.273
5 Champ. Series	16	60	6	16	3	0	1	6	.267
3 World Series	16	57	11	9	3	1	3	4	.158
All-Star Games	3	12	0	4	0	0	0	1	.333

VIC RASCHI

Career

Vic Raschi probably was the hardest working player of his time, always striving to squeeze the most from his natural ability. He had a great fastball, an average curveball, and more heart than anyone in baseball. On workdays Raschi would psyche himself to a fever pitch, glare at his own teammates, take the mound with an unshaven face, and scowl at intimidated hitters. Catcher Yogi Berra would needle him, making him madder and better. Vic battled every hitter he ever faced.

Lest you get the wrong idea, Raschi was not a crazy man. Off the field, Vic was quiet, conservative, responsible—and generally a nice guy. Sometimes he was too quiet for his own good and got short-changed in the publicity department.

Raschi's nickname, the Springfield Rifle, derived from Springfield, Massachusetts, where he was born in 1919. Yankee scout Gene McCann signed Raschi, who got a college scholarship in the deal and attended William and Mary. Vic broke into the Yankee farm system in 1941, going 10-6 at Amsterdam. Then came a year at Norfolk and three seasons in the military. He was with Binghamton and Newark in 1946 before getting called up to New York in September. He made two starts and won them both.

Raschi began 1947 with Portland, where he received excellent instruction from pitching coach Jim Turner and was 8-2 when the Yankees recalled him in July. He won the final game of a record 19-game Yankee winning streak. He finished with a 7-2 record and finally was a major leaguer at the age of 28.

Once he got to the big show, there was no stopping Raschi. Starting in 1948, he reeled off consecutive yearly records of 19-8, 21-10, 21-8, and 21-10. He never experienced a winning percentage of less than .677 in his eight Yankee seasons. His Yankee career winning percentage of .706 is the second highest among former Yankees with at least 100 decisions. Vic led the league with a .724 winning percentage in 1950 and won 11 consecutive games in 1952.

Raschi was a large right-hander (6'1" and 205 lbs) and a dependable workhorse. Besides completing almost 48 percent of his Yankee starts, Raschi never missed a starting assignment. And he played the latter part of his career with painfully damaged knees!

VIC RASCHI (United Press Telephoto — 2/26/52)

Raschi was a big-game pitcher and did some of his best work in October. In the opener of the 1950 World Series in Philadelphia, Raschi and Jim Konstanty hooked up in a tense game that the Yankees won, 1–0, Vic allowing only a pair of fifth-inning singles. He beat Brooklyn twice in the 1952 World Series.

Few pitchers have been more valuable to their club than Raschi was to the Yankees. His earned run averages were usually not spectacular for a simple reason: If Raschi had a big lead, he gave up some runs. If his teammates had trouble scoring, he held the opponent to fewer runs. After a 13–6 season in 1953, General Manager George Weiss demanded a big cut in Vic's salary. Raschi held out, as did several other Yankees that year, and in February of 1954, Weiss sent Raschi to the Cardinals. The rest of the players fell in line, but neither they nor Casey Stengel were happy about losing the gutsy Raschi, whose knees were badly damaged by then. Vic was a combined 12–16 in his final two years in the majors.

All-Star
Vic Raschi made the American League All-Star team in 1948–50 and in 1952. He was the winning pitcher in the 1948 game, pitching three scoreless frames over the middle innings and driving in the winning runs with a two-run single. The Americans won, 5–2, in St. Louis.

Over the last three innings of the 1949 game, Raschi held the National League scoreless, allowing only one hit. The Americans won, 11–7, in Brooklyn. The Springfield Rifle started the 1950 and 1952 games, with no decisions. The Nationals won both games.

Yankee Stats

	W	L	PCT	G	GS	CG	SA	SO	ERA
8 Years	120	50	.706	218	207	99	3	832	3.47
6 World Series	5	3	.625	11	8	3	0	43	2.24
All-Star Games	1	0	1.000	4	2	0	1	8	2.45

ALLIE REYNOLDS

Career

Part Creek Indian, Allie Reynolds was known as the Chief, the Big Chief, and Superchief. He broke into baseball's pro ranks in 1939, joined Cleveland three years later, and compiled a 51–47 record over five Indian seasons. In October of 1946, the Yankees dealt Joe Gordon to the Indians for their choice of one of several pitchers. Yankee brass leaned toward another pitcher, but followed Joe DiMaggio's advice and selected Reynolds.

The Big Chief was 19–8 for New York in 1947 and proved to be a vital acquisition; the Yanks drove to their first pennant in four years. He hurled shutouts in his first two starts and finished with a league-leading .704 winning percentage. He added a complete-game win against Brooklyn in the World Series. At the age of 32, Reynolds' career had skyrocketed; he would finish with a 182–107 lifetime record and a reputation as one of the most popular and intelligent Yankees ever.

Allie, who once said, "You get smart only when you begin getting old," was born in 1915 in Bethany, Oklahoma, and was a football star at Oklahoma A&M (now Oklahoma State) in the 1930s. The big, burly, right-handed fireballer was always one of the hardest throwers in the game, winning strikeout titles in 1943 with Cleveland and in 1952 with New York.

Known as a great "two-way pitcher," Reynolds was the best combination starter and reliever in Yankee history and, because of his versatility, was considered by many as the league's most valuable pitcher. In 86 Yankee relief appearances, Reynolds saved 41 games and won another 15. Superchief not only posted a 20–8 record with a league-leading 2.06 ERA in 1952, but saved six games in six relief appearances and was unscored upon. In 1953, he collected 20 relief points (seven relief wins and 13 saves), while suffering only one defeat in 26 relief appearances (he was 6–6 in 15 starts). Among all former Yankee pitchers, Allie's .686 winning percentage is lower than those of only Spud Chandler, Vic Raschi, and Whitey Ford.

Reynolds pitched 13 shutouts over the 1951–52 seasons, leading the league both years. His seven whitewashes in 1951, the most by a Yankee in 41 years, included two no-hitters. The first was a 1–0 masterpiece against Cleveland on July 12 and the second an 8–0 trouncing of Boston on September 28.

ALLIE REYNOLDS (AP Wirephoto)

Allie was at his best in October; he is tied for second in both World Series wins (seven) and saves (four). He made six relief appearances in World Series play and got either a save or a win in each. He batted .308 with eight hits, one less than Christy Mathewson, who holds the World Series record for hits by a pitcher. Ironically, when Allie joined the Yankees he had a reputation of being weak under pressure, a tag that Allie continually disproved in his eight Yankee seasons. Allie won or saved the final games of the 1950, 1952, and 1953 World Series.

Pitching effectively despite pain, he went 16–12 in 1950 with elbow chips in his right arm. Stengel said, "He's got lumps in his elbow the size of tangerines, but he's ready every time I call on him." In July of 1953, Reynolds hurt his back in an accident involving a bus carrying the Yankee team. The injury pained him over his final 1 1/2 seasons. He left baseball following the 1954 season.

All-Star
Allie Reynolds was a five-time All-Star. He pitched three innings and allowed only one hit in the 1950 game. He pitched the fourth and fifth innings of the 1953 game, allowing the game's first two runs and taking the defeat as the Nationals went on to a 5–1 victory in Cincinnati. Allie was an unused All-Star in 1949 and 1952. He was named to the 1954 team, at the age of 39, but was removed from the roster because of an injury.

Yankee Stats

	W	L	PCT	G	GS	CG	SA	SO	ERA
8 Years	131	60	.686	295	209	96	41	967	3.30
6 World Series	7	2	.778	15	9	5	4	62	2.79
All-Star Games	0	1	.000	2	0	0	0	2	3.60

BOBBY RICHARDSON

Career

Some thought that Bobby Richardson, a boyish 5'9", was too small for professional baseball, but H. P. Dawson, who ran New York's Norfolk club, signed him to a contract on the day Bobby graduated from high school. After breaking in slowly at Norfolk in 1953, Bobby was sent down to Olean and hit .412 in 32 games. A couple of years later he was with Denver, where, in 1956, he hit .328 under Manager Ralph Houk.

Richardson had brief trials with the Yankees in 1955–56 before making the big club for good in 1957. The second base job opened up. Bill Martin was traded and Jerry Coleman decided to retire. By 1959, Bobby was the first-string second baseman. And Robert Clinton Richardson—an activist Christian gentleman who was born in 1935 in Sumter, South Carolina, heart of the Bible Belt—held the job for eight seasons.

Richardson won five consecutive Gold Gloves as the league's best fielding second baseman, 1961–65. He had range and was quick, smooth, and sure. One of the most beautiful things in sports was the way Bobby turned a double play with shortstop Tony Kubek, especially when Bobby fielded the grounder. His feet planted, he'd shift to his right, his right knee would hit the ground as he'd fire a perfect throw to Kubek as Tony crossed the bag. Bobby led league second basemen four times in turning double plays.

Richardson was a solid batsman, who usually batted in the first or second slot, setting the table for bigger bats. He had good bat control and was a good bunter. He turned tiger in 1959, hitting .301, and again in 1962, when he hit .302, scored 99 runs, and rapped 38 doubles. Bobby also recorded 209 hits, the most by a Yankee since Red Rolfe's 213 hits in 1939. (No Yankee has since reached 200 hits.)

According to Brooks Robinson, Richardson was the best clutch hitter Robinson ever played against, and Brooks played from 1955 until 1977. Bobby had a record six RBIs in the third game of the 1960 World Series and a record 12 RBIs for the Series (after collecting only 26 RBIs in the regular season). He was *Sport* magazine's Series MVP and to this day remains the only member of a losing team to win that honor. Richardson had the game-winning hit in the 1964 pennant clincher and laced a record 13 hits in that year's World Series.

BOBBY RICHARDSON (Bob Olen)

He was reliable, getting into 150 or more games in each season from 1960 to 1965. He began 1966 with a unique five-year contract, calling for one year as a player and four years as a scout. He and Kubek had an agreement that they would not retire the same year."When Tony was forced to quit because of an injury, I came back for another year as I promised," said Bobby, who probably would have liked to retire in 1965. He hit .251 in 1966 and then retired at the age of 31. In 1970 the Yankees released Richardson from the final year of his contract so that he could become head baseball coach at the University of South Carolina.

All-Star
Bobby Richardson was a seven-time All-Star. He was selected but didn't play in the 1957 game, nor did he play in the second game in 1959. He was a replacement in both 1962 games, 1963, 1965, and 1966. Bobby started the 1964 game, won, 7–4, by the Nationals at Shea Stadium, and made one hit in four at bats.

Yankee Stats

	G	AB	R	H	2B	3B	HR	RBI	BA
12 Years	1,412	5,386	643	1,432	196	37	34	390	.266
7 World Series	36	131	16	40	6	2	1	15	.305
All-Star Games	6	11	1	1	0	0	0	0	.091

MICKEY RIVERS

Career

Mickey Rivers and Ed Figueroa, key pieces to New York's championship puzzle, came to the Yankees from California in a trade that sent
Bobby Bonds to the Angels. The deal was made in December of
1975, the year the speedy Rivers stole 70 bases. The exciting Mickey,
a product of Miami's Brownsville ghetto, had been a mischievous kid,
but not a bad one. Baseball kept him off the trouble-strewn streets
and carried him to the majors in 1970, the year Mickey broke in with
the Angels.

John Milton Rivers may have been the fastest speed merchant
ever to wear pinstripes. His slow, "Old Man River" stroll to the plate
was a comic contradiction of his blazing speed. "If I didn't know who
he was," Sparky Lyle said, "I'd figure he walked on hot coals for a
living." As a Yankee, Mickey was as quick as he was fast. On third
base when a thrown ball once trickled a few feet away from Doug
DeCinces, Rivers was crossing the plate almost before DeCinces
could pick up the ball. He was quick!

Mickey was 43-for-50 in the stolen base department in 1976,
pilfering more bases than any Yankee since Snuffy Stirnweiss stole
55 bases in 1944. In 1977, Mickey batted 565 times and grounded
into only two double plays, the latter tying Mickey Mantle's 1961
Yankee record. The fleet Mickey covered all of center field and his
less-than-powerful throwing arm never seemed to hurt the Yankee
cause. Mickey threw accurately and had a quick release; he'd
position his body perfectly in order to get all 165 pounds into his
throw.

The left-handed-swinging Rivers hit .312 and .326 in his first two
Yankee years and in the first of these, 1976, hit safely in 20 straight
games. He was a clutch hitter, batting .348, .391, and .455 in three
Championship Series against Kansas City, and an aggressive hitter.
Seldom did he walk.

The likable, happy-go-lucky Mickey called people "gozzleheads"
and "warpleheads" and loved playing cards and going to the race
track. But when money matters weighed heavy (Mickey didn't think
he was making enough on the Yankees), he could become moody
and play with rationed enthusiasm. Finally, in July of 1979, the Yanks
dealt him to Texas. Mickey, who in 1980 stroked 210 hits, currently is
one of the most quoted ballplayers. Early in 1983, Mickey spoke of

being reunited with George Steinbrenner and Billy Martin if a rumored trade to the Yankees were to materialize. Said Mick the Quick, "Me and George and Billy are two of a kind."

All-Star
Mickey Rivers was an All-Star in the 1976 game, which the Nationals won, 7–1, in Philadelphia. He entered as a pinch hitter, struck out, and took over in right field. He later singled.

Yankee Stats

	G	AB	R	H	2B	3B	HR	RBI	BA
4 Years	490	2,000	289	598	92	26	34	209	.299
3 Champ. Series	14	57	10	22	2	1	0	2	.386
3 World Series	15	63	4	15	2	0	0	2	.238
All-Star Games	1	2	0	1	0	0	0	0	.500

MICKEY RIVERS (NY Yankees)

PHIL RIZZUTO

Career

Phil Rizzuto, barely five feet tall upon graduation from Brooklyn's Richmond Hill High School, tried out for the Brooklyn Dodgers and New York Giants; both organizations told him he was too small. The Yankees, meanwhile, ran their very first tryout program at Yankee Stadium. Rizzuto attended several workouts, impressed Joe McCarthy and head scout Paul Krichell, and was signed. General Manager Ed Barrow figured it cost the Yanks 15 or 20 cents to sign Rizzuto—the price of a sandwich and a bottle of milk the Yanks gave him after his final workout.

The Brooklyn-reared Rizzuto, who was born September 25, 1918, entered a whole new world with his first minor league assignment in Virginia. He did well at Bassett and Norfolk and hit .347 at Kansas City in 1940, the year Phil was named the Minor League Player of the Year. Rizzuto and Jerry Priddy formed one of the greatest double-play combinations in bush league history. Teammate Billy Hitchcock, who marveled at how Rizzuto scooted after grounders, began calling him "Scooter" and the nickname took.

Rizzuto and Priddy were to become New York's new double-play combination in 1941, but Priddy didn't stick. It was a rough spring for little Scooter, the Yankee veterans not exactly welcoming him with open arms. Scooter was replacing incumbent shortstop Frank Crosetti, a popular member of the cast, and it was well after Opening Day that Joe DiMaggio broke the ice and became the first Yankee to speak to Phil. The other players would soon join in—it wasn't all that hard to accept a rookie who hit .307 in 133 games.

In Rizzuto's 13-season Yankee career (he spent the 1943–45 seasons in the navy), he played 1,647 games at shortstop and two at second base. He was durable. The spark plug on 10 pennant winners and eight World Championship clubs, Phil, at 5'6" and 150 or so pounds, was the favorite of many Yankee fans. He was an underdog hero on a team loaded with premier players. The little guy with no muscles won with intelligence and by taking every edge given him. His favorite manager, Joe McCarthy, said, "For a little fellow to beat a big fellow he has to be terrific, he has to have everything, and Rizzuto's got it."

PHIL RIZZUTO (NY Yankees)

No one fielded better at shortstop than Rizzuto. Not before or since. Scooter made the most difficult plays look easy, saving game after game with his defensive artistry. He was quick and fast, graceful and acrobatic.

Rizzuto ranks in the top 10 among history's shortstops with 1,217 double plays, and he could start them or turn them with equal skill and beauty. In fielding grounders near second, Phil was adept with the shovel pass or backhand flip to the second baseman. In receiving the throw, Phil would leap high into the air with his knees bent for protection, squarely face the first baseman, and snap a strong throw from behind his right ear. He led American League shortstops in fielding average in 1949 and 1950.

Rizzuto was an expert at handling the bat, hitting to all fields and hitting behind the runner. He was a superb bunter, perhaps the best ever, and he led the majors in sacrifices four years in a row (1949–52). He was a master at faking the bunt, swinging away and knocking the ball past the charging first baseman. His best season with the stick was 1950, the year he was the league's MVP, when he collected 200 hits and batted .324. He scored 125 runs that year.

Just as Jackie Robinson terrorized the National League with his baserunning, the Scooter was the scourge of his league as the best and most daring baserunner. He had good speed, and could start and stop almost as quickly as Robinson. His career high in stolen bases was only 22, but he had amazing stolen-base percentages, such as .857 in 1951, when he stole 18 bases in 21 attempts. He ranks ninth on New York's all-time stolen-base list with 149 and third on the World Series list with 10.

Rizzuto achieved greatness in spite of several phobias. He was (and is) afraid of flying, storms, and anything that crawls. Teammates loved to put creepy things in his glove between innings. Phil responded by becoming one of the first players to bring his glove to the dugout when his team was at bat. But his teammates loved Rizzuto and went to great lengths to protect him on the field, although little Phil was actually fearless on the diamond and took his lumps with the best of them.

Phil and Stan Musial were rated by Ty Cobb in 1951 as the only two midcentury players who could have starred in Cobb's era. They played the same all-round game that Ty Cobb knew. Without question, Rizzuto was the greatest all-round shortstop in Yankee history. But he has been continually snubbed by Baseball Hall of Fame voters, who seem to undervalue team play, fielding, bunting, and baserunning. And, holy cow, how many shortstops have had a career .273 average?

Rizzuto, who was released by the Yankees on Old Timers' Day in 1956, joined Mel Allen and Red Barber in the Yankee broadcast booth in 1957, and in 1983 he began his 27th season announcing Yankee games. Phil enjoys even greater popularity than in his great playing days, and he was an immensely popular player.

All-Star

Phil Rizzuto was a five-time All-Star, gaining selection in 1942 (although he didn't play) and 1950–53. Phil started and played all of the 1950 and 1952 games. He was the leadoff man in 1950 and went 2-for-6, but the Nationals won, 4–3, in 14 innings at Chicago's Comiskey Park. The Scooter went hitless in two trips in a rain-shortened, five-inning 1952 game at Philadelphia's Shibe Park that was won by the Nationals, 3–2.

Yankee Stats

	G	AB	R	H	2B	3B	HR	RBI	BA
13 Years	1,661	5,816	877	1,588	239	62	38	562	.273
9 World Series	52	183	21	45	3	0	2	8	.246
All-Star Games	4	9	0	2	0	0	0	0	.222

AARON ROBINSON

Career

Aaron Robinson was the short-span bridge between New York's catcher immortals, Bill Dickey—who caught through 1943, entered military service, and was succeeded by a number of backstops before Robinson settled into the slot—and Yogi Berra. Aaron became the main man behind the plate in 1946, and in 1947 split the receiving duties with Berra. In February of 1948, he and two pitchers were traded to the White Sox for Eddie Lopat. The Yankee catching job was Berra's. Robinson completed an eight-year big league career in 1951 with a .260 lifetime average.

Big Aaron (6'2", 205 lbs) was a country boy out of Camp Creek Township, in Lancaster County, South Carolina. He raised and tamed gamecocks and played "town ball" as a lad, advancing to the competitive semi-pro leagues in the Carolinas. Aaron was a third baseman, the position he played even after signing with the Yankees.

Robby spent seven years in the Yankee farm chain, his progress retarded by injuries, but eventually climbed from Class-D Snow Hill to Newark and finally to New York for one game in 1943 (at the age of 28). Then he entered the Coast Guard, where he served until July of 1945, when he returned to the Yanks and hit .281 without making an error in 45 games behind the plate.

In 1946, Yankee Manager Dickey turned over the first-string catching job to Robinson, who caught in 95 games to Dickey's 39. A left-handed hitter, Aaron could drive the baseball. He hit 16 home runs in 1946 with 64 RBIs in 330 at bats. His .297 average was the highest among the club's regulars and was seven points higher than DiMaggio's. Robinson was clearly the outstanding slugging catcher in baseball and made the postseason major league All-Star team picked by *The Sporting News*.

Aaron caught 74 games in 1947 while Berra, who was in his first full campaign, handled 51 (and played another 25 games in the outfield). Robinson hit a respectable .270. But the Yanks' future hopes were pinned to the Yog.

All-Star

Aaron Robinson was passed over as an All-Star selection in 1946, his greatest season, but he made the team for the 1947 game. He rode the bench, however, while Buddy Rosar of the A's caught the entire game, won by the Americans, 2–1.

Yankee Stats

	G	AB	R	H	2B	3B	HR	RBI	BA
4 Years	233	743	74	211	34	8	29	124	.284
1 World Series	3	10	2	2	0	0	0	1	.200

All-Star Games (no appearances)

AARON ROBINSON (NY Yankees)

RED ROLFE

Career

He may have looked like a Turkey Creek product, but Red Rolfe was actually an Ivy Leaguer. Born in Penacook, New Hampshire, on October 17, 1908, Robert Abial Rolfe had great baseball careers at Exeter and Dartmouth. He was signed by Yankee scout Paul Krichell in 1931 and that year hit .336 at Albany (and played one game at New York). He starred at shortstop in Newark in 1932–33, hitting .333 and .328, respectively. Newark Manager Al Mamaux said in Red's first year with the Bears that he had never seen a player improve as rapidly as Red. The next year several big league clubs wanted Rolfe, Brooklyn supposedly offering $50,000 plus players for him. But Yankee owner Jacob Ruppert would make no deal.

Rolfe made the Yankees in 1934. Manager Joe McCarthy felt Red really didn't have the arm to play shortstop; besides, Frank Crosetti, who did have a great arm, was entrenched there. Yet McCarthy liked Red's glove and foresaw third base as Rolfe's permanent home. Joe broke Red in slowly, alternating him at both positions in 1934.

Rolfe became New York's regular third baseman in 1935 and held the job for seven seasons. He made a remarkably quick transition, leading the league's third basemen in fielding in 1935 and 1936. He was exactly the type of undemonstrative, efficient and disciplined ballplayer McCarthy craved. He was so quiet that he sometimes got lost among his famous teammates, and he was indeed the unheralded star of the team. He knew his job, worked hard at it without a lot of fanfare, and was greatly respected by his teammates. He was a dedicated gentleman off the field and a determined competitor on it.

The left-handed-hitting redhead had tremendous offensive punch even though he wasn't much with the home run. But he had excellent extra-base power. Over the 1936–39 seasons (all World Championship years), he netted 64, 48, 54, and 70 extra-base hits, an amazing total considering he had only 38 combined homers. And Red hit .300 four times in both regular season and World Series play. His best season was 1939 when he hit .329, played in all 152 Yankee games, and led the league with 213 hits, 46 doubles, and 139 runs scored. No Yankee player has since surpassed his figures in any of the three league-leading categories.

Rolfe was one of the most prolific run-scorers in Yankee history. In his seven years as a regular, he averaged 120.85 runs per season.

Once, in 1935, he scored eight runs in a doubleheader. He owns one of the more impressive American League records, set in August of 1939, when he scored at least one run in 18 consecutive games.

After hitting .219 as a part-time third baseman in 1942, Rolfe retired to coach baseball and basketball at Yale. He managed Detroit from 1949 to 1952 and did a remarkable job with the mediocre Tigers, especially in 1950 when he brought them home second, only three games behind the Yankees.

All-Star

Red Rolfe was an All·Star four years running, from 1937 through 1940. He was a starter in the 1937 game, which his team won in Washington, 8–3. He committed two errors but went 2-for-4 as leadoff man, scoring two runs and getting a two-run triple off Carl Hubbell. He started the 1939 game before the home folks at Yankee Stadium, getting one hit in four trips in the Americans' 3–1 triumph. Red didn't play in the 1938 or 1940 games.

Yankee Stats

	G	AB	R	H	2B	3B	HR	RBI	BA
10 Years	1,175	4,827	942	1,394	257	67	69	497	.289
6 World Series	?8	116	17	33	4	1	0	6	.284
All-Star Games	2	8	2	3	0	1	0	2	.375

RED ROLFE

BUDDY ROSAR

Career

Warren Vincent "Buddy" Rosar was discovered by the boss's wife. Mrs. Joe McCarthy saw him playing in an amateur all-star game in hometown Buffalo in 1934 and described the 20-year-old to Marse Joe as an outstanding catching prospect. McCarthy passed the word along to Yankee scout Gene McCann and subsequently Rosar was signed.

Rosar played at Wheeling, Norfolk, and Binghamton; in 1937 he reached Newark where he spent two seasons, hitting .332 and .387. Up with the Yankees in 1939, he hit .276 as Bill Dickey's backup catcher and remained Dickey's caddy for four seasons, playing brilliantly whenever he got the chance—usually in the late innings or in the second game of a doubleheader.

Rosar, stockily built at 5'9" and 190 pounds, was a strong defensive catcher. Many felt he was the best in the game. He was especially good at handling throws in the dirt, whether from a pitcher or an outfielder. Catching for the Philadelphia A's in 1946, Buddy played 121 games as catcher and fielded a perfect 1.000, a big league record.

Buddy hit .261 over 13 major league seasons (1939–51). He hit his career high of .298 with the Yankees in 1940 and had two incredible back-to-back days at the Stadium that season against Cleveland. He hit a first-inning grand-slam homer as the Yankees won, 9–6, on July 18, and the next day hit for the cycle as New York won again, 15–6. Two homers in two days—and Buddy hit only 18 lifetime.

He finally got his big break when Dickey went down with an injury in July of 1942. But he defied management by traveling to Buffalo to take a police candidate's exam. He reasoned that baseball's future was uncertain because of the war and felt he had to make arrangements to provide for his family. The Yankees didn't like his reasoning at all; they fined him $250 when he rejoined the club three days later and in December dealt him to Cleveland. Buddy had several outstanding years with the Indians, Athletics, and Red Sox. There were occasional rumors that the Yanks might reobtain him, but these never materialized.

All-Star

As a Yankee, Buddy Rosar made the 1942 American League All-Star team, along with Bill Dickey, but Birdie Tebbetts caught the entire

game. Rosar was also an All-Star with Cleveland (once) and with
Philadelphia (three times).

Yankee Stats

	G	AB	R	H	2B	3B	HR	RBI	BA
4 Years	252	751	95	205	43	6	7	119	.273
2 World Series	2	1	0	1	0	0	0	0	1.000

All-Star Games (no appearances)

BUDDY ROSAR (NY Yankees)

RED RUFFING

Career

Known to baseball fans as Red and to his friends as Charley, Charles Herbert Ruffing became one of baseball's greatest pitchers only after overcoming a physical handicap.

Ruffing was born May 3, 1904, in Granville, Illinois. When he was 15, he went to work with his father in the Nokomis, Illinois, coal mines. The elder Ruffing doubled as manager of the company baseball team for which Red, a great power hitter, played. In 1921, Red lost four toes on his left foot in a mining accident. Unable to run well enough to play the outfield, he quit baseball for a year. But then he came back to the game, trying his luck on the mound, where running ability isn't so important. He discovered he could balance his damaged foot without much difficulty, and he was back in business.

In 1923, Ruffing entered professional baseball with Danville. His contract was purchased by the Red Sox at the end of the season and in 1924 he went 0–0 for Boston. Pitching for the worst Red Sox teams in the club's history, Red's records beginning in 1925 were 9–18, 6–15, 5–13, 10–25, and 9–22. Boston finished last in each of those years. For his part, Red had some great moments, like the time he struck out Babe Ruth, Lou Gehrig, and Bob Meusel on just 10 pitches. His contract was acquired in May of 1930 in a deal that required the Yanks to send outfielder Cedric Durst (in his last big league season) and $50,000 to Boston.

Ruffing became the greatest right-hander in Yankee history, producing a winning record over 14 of his 15 Yankee seasons. He won more games, started and completed more games, pitched in more games, and struck out more batters than any other Yankee right-hander. Between 1930 and 1942, he and Lefty Gomez combined to win 408 Yankee games. Over the 1936–39 seasons, when the Yankees became the first club to win four consecutive World Championships, Ruffing went 20–12, 20–7, 21–7, and 21–7 for a combined 82–33 record. He is the only Yankee 20-game winner over four consecutive seasons.

Rufus the Red was tough in October. Only Whitey Ford has more World Series wins (10) than Ruffing's seven. He started six World Series openers and won five of them to get the Yanks off and running. He won two games in the four-game sweep of the Cubs in 1938. In the first game of the 1942 Series, he pitched hitless ball for 7 2/3 innings.

At 6'2" and 205 pounds, Ruffing was both strong and durable. He pitched 200 or more innings in 13 consecutive seasons (1928–40), tying Eddie Plank's league record; his 261 complete games as a Yankee is a club record—and 88 more than second-place Lefty Gomez. He was a basic pitcher, coming at hitters with a smoking fastball and a curveball—nothing fancy—adding to these a change-up he developed in 1932. He was a rugged competitor, who paced himself so that he always had plenty of stuff left for the late innings. His lifetime ERA of 3.80 may seem high, but Red pitched in an age when sluggers ruled the American League.

Ruffing was a great hitter, batting .269 lifetime but hitting better than .300 eight times, with a high of .364 in 1930. He holds the big league RBI record for a pitcher with 273, one for each of his 273 big league wins. He hit 36 career homers, had two two-homer games, and in 1933 became the first Yankee pitcher to hit a grand-slam homer. On August 13, 1932, he put on an impressive one-man show against Washington, allowing three hits, striking out 10, and belting a 10th-inning homer to win, 1–0. He was seldom lifted for a pinch hitter; in fact, he was often used as a pinch hitter. In effect, Red held two jobs on the Yanks. Red made 58 career pinch hits and in 1935 hit .444 (8-for-18) as a pinch hitter to lead the majors.

Ruffing was well read, intelligent, and articulate. He was a shrewd contract negotiator. And he was all business on the mound, giving some fans the impression that he was exclusively business—a humorless cold fish. But Red, while no Gomez or Dizzy Dean in the color department, was a regular guy who liked to horse around with his teammates.

Ruffing entered military service in December of 1942 and wasn't released from the Army Air Corps until June of 1945. He was some 30 pounds overweight and 41 years old. Yet he got himself into shape and on July 26, 1945, pitched six shutout innings against the A's in a remarkable initial performance. He finished the season at 7–3. He won his first five decisions in 1946, but suffered a loss and broken kneecap in the same game and was out for the year. In September, New York released Ruffing, who pitched for the White Sox in 1947 and retired after 22 great seasons in the majors. Twenty years later, in 1967, Red was inducted into the Baseball Hall of Fame.

All-Star

Red Ruffing was a six-time All-Star. He was shelled in the 1934 game, giving up four hits and three runs in one inning, plus four batters. He didn't pitch in the 1938, 1941, or 1942 games.

Ruffing made consecutive All-Star starts in 1939 and 1940. The 1939 game was played at Yankee Stadium and Red permitted only one run and fanned four in a three-inning stint. He didn't get the decision but the Americans won, 3–1. The following year, Red got off to a rocky start in St. Louis, the first two batters singling and Max West blasting a three-run homer. They were the only runs Red allowed in three innings, but he took the loss, the Nationals winning, 4–0.

Yankee Stats

	W	L	PCT	G	GS	CG	SA	SO	ERA
15 Years	231	124	.651	426	391	261	8	1,526	3.47
7 World Series	7	2	.778	10	10	7	0	61	2.63
All-Star Games	0	1	.000	3	2	0	0	6	9.00

RED RUFFING

MARIUS RUSSO

Career

Marius Russo might have taken his place with the all-time Yankee mound greats had it not been for arm troubles. The Brooklyn native who was signed out of Long Island University, where he was better known as a basketball player, posted an 8–8 record for Newark in 1937 and the next year went 17–8. He was still with the Bears when 1939 began, but was called up to New York in mid-season.

The 25-year-old was the best young left-hander in baseball in 1939. He entered his first Yankee game in relief and, with two outs and the bases full of Indians, notched a sidearm strikeout. Showing poise and coolness under pressure throughout his rookie year, Marius finished with an 8–3 record and with nine complete games in 11 starts.

He went 14–8 in 1940 and 14–10 in 1941 as the Yankees' top southpaw over those campaigns. On June 26, 1941, he hurled a one-hitter against the Browns, allowing only a seventh-inning homer by George McQuinn. He beat the Dodgers, 2–1, at Ebbets Field in the critical third game of the 1941 World Series, helping himself by knocking out pitching rival Freddie Fitzsimmons with a line drive off Freddie's leg. He was a finesse pitcher with good control. He had a curveball, a change of pace and a sneaky quick fastball, and he mixed up his pitches well.

Russo hurt his arm in May of 1942, reinjured it in August, and that year got into only nine games. The arm problems continued over the 1943 season when Russo went 5–10. However, Marius pitched well down the stretch and Manager Joe McCarthy gave him a starting assignment in the World Series against the Cardinals. He pitched a seven-hitter, got nicked for only one unearned run, and scored the winning run in a 2–1 victory. McCarthy got a kick out of Russo's excellent performance, what with some people questioning his judgment in starting Marius. But it would prove to be Russo's final big league win.

Russo was in the military over the 1944–45 seasons, and in January of 1946 had bone chips removed from his pitching elbow. He was 0–2 in August of 1946, went down to the Kansas City farm, and never reached the majors again.

All-Star

Marius Russo was selected to the American League All-Star team in 1941. The Americans used four pitchers in their 7–5 victory in Detroit, but Russo wasn't one of them.

Yankee Stats

	W	L	PCT	G	GS	CG	SA	SO	ERA
6 Years	45	34	.570	120	84	48	5	311	3.13
2 World Series	2	0	1.000	2	2	2	0	7	0.50

All-Star Games (no appearances)

MARIUS RUSSO (NY Yankees)

Career

Joe Dugan, recalling teammate Babe Ruth: "He was unique. There was nobody like him . . . there was never anybody close. He was a god." He was, indeed, something of a god; his was a time of gods, a time when every sport had one, the 1920s—the Golden Age of Sports. And Ruth reigned supreme among them. He was magnificent. He was more than charismatic; he was magnetic. And yet, if there ever was a man, a genuine earthling, it was Babe Ruth. The wondrous heroics and achievements of Babe Ruth belong to humankind, and with them go the insatiable appetites, the excesses, and the conflicts of a battling, indulging, fun-loving, and fun-providing *man*.

George Herman Ruth was born February 6, 1895, to saloon-keeping Baltimoreans. "I was a bad kid. I say that without pride." is the way Ruth opened his autobiography. He ended up in Baltimore's St. Mary's Industrial School for Boys, where he learned to play baseball—well. Jack Dunn, owner of the International League's Baltimore Orioles, signed Ruth and in the spring of 1914 young George joined the Orioles. The veterans called the 19-year-old "Dunn's Babe," the source of his famous nickname.

The Babe was 6'2″ and 185 pounds, a far cry from the overweight 260-pounder he would later become. He pitched for Baltimore, and later, when Dunn sold his contract to the Red Sox, he worked for Providence and Boston. Beginning the next year, 1915, he won 18, 23, and 24 games over three seasons and was the league's best left-hander. But the Red Sox, wanting the Babe's big bat in the lineup daily, in 1918 began playing Ruth in the outfield. Ruth would finish his mound work with a lifetime 2.28 ERA and a won-loss record of 94–46, including a 5–0 mark with the Yankees.

The Yankees took the big step toward becoming the celebrated Yankees (or the damn Yankees, depending on your viewpoint) shortly after Christmas in 1919 when they bought Ruth's contract. With Ruth they won their first seven pennants. Ruth made them the most famous sports franchise in the world. New York City was the perfect stage for Ruth, who put so many people into the Polo Grounds that the Yankees in 1923 could confidently open Yankee Stadium, "the House that Ruth built." Babe was the Bambino and the Sultan of Swat, and because of him, the Yankees stole the Big Apple away from the Giants.

Babe Ruth turned the game of baseball around. He brought to it the longball. Until 1919, the year Ruth hit 29 homers to set his first home run record, major league teams relied on bunting, place hitting, stolen bases, and the hit-and-run play, the "inside baseball" made successful by John J. McGraw. But with Babe showing the way (and the lively ball's introduction in 1920), baseball became a power game. By putting balls into orbit, Ruth saved professional baseball at a time when the Black Sox scandal threatened to mire the game in the muck of public-betraying gambling.

Ruth was a complete ballplayer. He was a fine outfielder with a rifle arm and he ran the bases with speed and daring, stealing home 10 times and twice stealing 17 bases in one season. He always put his team's welfare first.

But what distinguished the Babe was his power hitting. He would hit booming, towering home runs, one of them reportedly traveling 602 feet. He copied the batting techniques of Shoeless Joe Jackson, but his home run trot was all his own. Grinning from ear to ear, he would circle the bases with baby steps, tipping his cap to the crowd, and occasionally throwing in a bow. He was a crowd pleaser. "I could have hit a .600 lifetime average easy," he said. "But I would have had to hit them singles. The people were paying to see me hit them home runs."

Some of Ruth's most famous records have fallen. Hank Aaron hit 755 lifetime homers to top Babe's 714. Roger Maris hit 61 homers in 1961 to top Babe's 60 in 1927. Mickey Mantle hit 18 World Series homers to top Babe's 15. Whitey Ford pitched 33 2/3 consecutive scoreless innings in World Series play to top Babe's 29 2/3, accomplished as a Red Sox pitcher. Yet, the Sultan of Swat still holds numerous records:

- Home Runs—Led league most seasons (12) . . . Most seasons with 40 or more (11) and 50 or more (4) . . . Most times to hit two or more in one game (72) . . . Most hit in one month (17, September of 1927) . . . Highest lifetime ratio (11.7).
- Slugging Average—Led league most seasons (13) . . . Owns the three highest in history (.847, 1920; .846, 1921; and .772, 1927) . . . Highest lifetime (.690).
- Bases on Balls—Led league most seasons (11) . . . Most in one season (190, 1923) . . . Most lifetime (2,056).

Babe hit for extra-base power *and* got on base consistently. For example, he established standing records in 1921 with 457 total

BABE RUTH (Bob Olen)

bases and 119 extra-base hits. Two years later he made 205 hits and drew 170 walks, his combined total of 375 outdistancing his nearest competitor (Ted Williams in 1949) by 19.

Ruth's records go on and on. But Babe did much more with a stick than hit 714 home runs. He hit .342 lifetime for one. In 1923, he hit the highest average in Yankee history (.393) and the following year he won the batting crown (.378). Ruth led the league in either homers, runs, RBIs, walks, batting, or slugging a total of 51 times!

The Bambino saved some of his best hitting for the World Series, and he hit better than .300 in six of seven of them as a Yankee. He hit the highest average in Series history, .625 in 1928, and twice belted three homers in a single Series game. Babe's most famous moment was his "called shot" homer against the Cubs in the 1932 Series. The ball landed near the top of the old center-field bleachers at Wrigley Field, right where the Bambino had gestured he would park one.

The Babe chased life's pleasures like they were fly balls. He had big appetites, spent loads of money, and drove fast cars. He was a carouser and spent little time in his hotel room. Overindulgence caught up with him in the spring of 1925, when he was stricken with "the bellyache heard 'round the world." He was sick for most of the spring and bothered by poor health the entire season.

When Robert Creamer was researching his book, *Babe: The Legend Comes to Life*, he poked around for a negative comment from Bob Shawkey, Ruth's manager in 1930. Instead, Shawkey said, "People sometimes got mad at him, but I never heard of anybody who didn't *like* Babe Ruth." When Red Ruffing and Lefty Gomez (future Hall of Famers) complained of the weight of liquor bags they were lugging for the Babe, Ruth told them, "You ought to be glad you could carry the bottles for old Baby." And they were. Everyone loved the Babe, both for himself and for what he had done for baseball and baseball salaries. He blew the salary ceiling out of sight with his $80,000 salary in 1930, explaining, when a reporter asked if he thought it right that he make more money than the president, "I had a better year than he did." The kids especially liked him and he in turn would do anything for them. He hit homers for sick kids, visited them in hospitals, and never sought any publicity for it.

But, as Shawkey said, people sometimes got mad at Ruth. Most often they were people in authority. Late in 1921, Babe defied Commissioner Landis, went on a barnstorming tour, and got a six-week suspension to begin the 1922 season. When he returned to action, Babe kept American League President Ban Johnson busy handing out more suspensions, usually for Babe's brushes with umpires. Ruth had five suspensions in 1922. (Break that record, Hank Aaron!) He battled with Yankee Manager Miller Huggins in 1925 and openly flouted club rules on a road trip, for which Huggins slapped him with a $5,000 fine.

Ruth badly wanted to manage the Yankees after Huggins died in 1929. But Shawkey and then Joe McCarthy got the job. After the 1934 season, he made one final pitch for the job, but Jacob Ruppert and Ed Barrow were pleased with McCarthy. In February of 1935, Ruppert, seeking nothing in return, released the 40-year-old Ruth to the Boston Braves. But Ruth remained a Brave only until June and then retired.

At home in New York City, Ruth enjoyed life and waited for a call to manage a major league club. Sadly, that call never came. He coached for Brooklyn in 1938 and kept close to baseball circles. After he was stricken with cancer, the Yankees held several days in his honor, and when he died in 1948, more than 100,000 people filed past his body at Yankee Stadium . . . the House that Ruth built. The entire nation mourned the loss of the famed, fabled, big-spirited Babe Ruth, charter member of the Baseball Hall of Fame and the greatest of all American sports heroes.

All-Star

Babe Ruth was a starting right fielder for the junior circuit in the first two years of the All-Star Game, 1933–34. He stole the show at Comiskey Park in 1933, delivering two hits, including the first homer in All-Star history, a third-inning two-run blast off Bill Hallahan. Ruth also made the best fielding play, spearing an eighth-inning liner off the bat of Chick Hafey. The Americans won, 4–2. In the 1934 game, played at the Polo Grounds, Ruth went hitless in two official trips but scored a run. The Americans won, 9–7.

Yankee Stats

	G	AB	R	H	2B	3B	HR	RBI	BA
15 Years	2,084	7,217	1,959	2,518	424	106	659	1,970	.349
7 World Series	36	118	37	41	5	1	15	30	.347
All-Star Games	2	6	2	2	0	0	1	2	.333

JOHNNY SAIN

Career

Johnny Sain didn't become a major leaguer overnight. He spent four years in the Class-D Northeast Arkansas League and even had trouble sticking with that lowly circuit. He had no velocity. In his seventh year in baseball, 1942, Sain reached the bigs as a relief pitcher with the Boston Braves, then managed by Casey Stengel. Next it was three years in the navy, then back to the Braves in 1946 and to the breaking balls and slow stuff Johnny was forced to rely on.

But things would turn around for Johnny Sain, by then 29. He would be a 20-game winner in four out of five seasons. He would team with Warren Spahn and in Boston they would say "Spahn and Sain and Pray for Rain."

When Stengel learned in 1951 that Sain, who was 5–13 at the time, was available, he asked George Weiss to obtain him. And so the Yanks did, sending young Lew Burdette and $50,000 to Boston in exchange for Johnny. Making his first Yankee start on Labor Day, Johnny beat the Athletics on a five-hitter, and six days later again started and claimed a second key win for New York.

In 1952–53, Sain was a swingman, making 35 starts and 40 relief appearances. He was 11–6 in 1952 and led the Yankee bullpen with seven saves. Johnny won the pennant clincher in relief. The next year Johnny went 14–7 and won the opening game of the World Series against Brooklyn in relief.

Sain's best Yankee season was 1954. His record fell to 6–6, but he led the league with 22 saves, setting the Yankee right-hander record that stood until Lindy McDaniel recorded 29 saves in 1970. Stengel used Sain in 45 games, all in relief. Sain also hit .353 (6-for-17).

The Yankees traded Sain to the Kansas City A's in May of 1955, his final major league season; Johnny finished at 139–116. He embarked on a long career as one of the game's greatest pitching coaches. He coached the Yankees over the pennant-winning seasons of 1961–63.

All-Star

Johnny Sain was a two-time National League All-Star, pitching in the 1947 and 1948 games. As a Yankee he was an American League All-Star in 1953 but didn't pitch in the game won by the Nationals, 5–1.

Yankee Stats

	W	L	PCT	G	GS	CG	SA	SO	ERA
5 Years	33	20	.623	130	39	19	39	200	3.32
3 World Series	1	1	.500	4	0	0	0	6	4.61
All-Star Games (no appearances)									

JOHNNY SAIN (NY Yankees)

GEORGE SELKIRK

Career

George Selkirk, perhaps unfairly remembered chiefly as the man who replaced Babe Ruth in right field, was an outstanding major leaguer in his own right.

Born in Huntsville, Ontario, in 1908, George broke into pro ball in 1927 with Jersey City where, after running out an inside-the-park homer in his own inimitable fashion, he was tagged "Twinkletoes." The Yankees assumed control of Selkirk's contract and discouraging times followed for Twinkletoes, who opened with Newark in 1932 and 1933 and then played for other International League clubs on a loan basis. In the 1933 International League playoffs, Selkirk, playing for Rochester, almost single-handedly defeated Newark. He was hitting .358 at Newark in August of 1934 when the Yankees sent for the 26-year-old Canadian. George was the heir apparent to the 39-year-old Ruth and in 46 games hit .313, 25 points higher than the Bambino.

With Ruth having departed, Selkirk was the Yankees' right fielder in 1935. The press sounded the Selkirk-replaces-Ruth theme, but Manager Joe McCarthy told George to forget the Ruth angle and concentrate on helping the club his own way. Selkirk, who wore Babe's No. 3 uniform, heard boos at first from Babe's legion of supporters, but he handled the pressure well and in time won over most of the boobirds. The fact that George had a great 1935 didn't hurt him; he was second on the club in RBIs (94) and average (.312).

Selkirk was an excellent hitter, batting over .300 in his first four Yankee seasons, five times in all. His .290 lifetime average ranks among the top 20 in Yankee history. His most productive seasons were 1936 (18 homers and 107 RBIs) and 1939 (21 homers and 101 RBIs). He had a great batting eye, walking more than 80 times three separate seasons, with a high of 103 in 1939.

Selkirk enjoyed several memorable days. He drove in eight runs in a single game twice, and in 1941 hit the first pinch-hit grand-slam homer in Yankee history. He became the fourth man to homer in his first World Series at bat, when he went downtown in the first game of the 1936 Series.

Selkirk was New York's regular right fielder until he broke his collarbone in 1937. That year, playing in only 78 games, he batted .328 and slugged .629, both career highs. In 1938 he switched to left field, played there regularly for three years, and led the league's outfielders with a .989 fielding percentage in 1939. Competition was enormous for jobs in the Yankees' talented outfield, especially after Tommy Henrich joined the club in 1937 and Charlie Keller made the scene in 1939. Selkirk more than held his own, but it once took him six weeks to reclaim his job after leaving a game with an injury.

After two years as a reserve outfielder, Selkirk's major league playing career, all with New York, ended when he entered the navy following the 1942 season. When he got out in 1946, he was 38 and went to Newark as manager. He handled other positions in the Yankee organization, then moved on to other clubs. He was general manager of Washington in the 1960s and made several great trades to build up the Senators, who were moving in the right direction when Selkirk stepped down.

All-Star

George Selkirk was an All-Star in 1936 and 1939. He walked as a pinch hitter in the 1936 game. In the 1939 game, played at Yankee Stadium and won by the Americans, 3–1, Selkirk started in left field and knocked in the tying run with a fourth-inning single.

Yankee Stats

	G	AB	R	H	2B	3B	HR	RBI	BA
9 Years	846	2,790	503	810	131	41	108	576	.290
6 World Series	21	68	11	18	2	1	2	10	.265
All-Star Games	2	2	0	1	0	0	0	1	.500

GEORGE SELKIRK

BOBBY SHANTZ

Career

Only 5'6" and less than 140 pounds, pitcher Bobby Shantz served an assortment of big-breaking curveballs and off-speed pitches. He was crafty in the mold of fellow left-hander Eddie Lopat, and he was one of the game's greatest fielding pitchers. He was the first Yankee to win a Gold Glove and he won four in a row, 1957–60.

Shantz was born in 1925 in Pottstown, Pennsylvania, and in 1948 broke into professional baseball. In 1949, working for the Philadelphia A's, he hurled nine innings of no-hit relief in only his second big league game. He won 24 games and the MVP Award in 1952, but late in that campaign fractured his wrist in the first of what was to be a succession of injuries. The next spring Bobby pulled tendons in his shoulder and would pitch in pain the rest of his career.

Shantz won only 13 games from 1953 to 1956 but had always given the Yankees trouble. So in February of 1957, when the Yankees concocted a multi-player deal with the A's, then in Kansas City, Yankee General Manager George Weiss was willing to gamble by taking Bobby as a throw-in. Then Bobby turned out to be the indispensable Yankee of 1957. He made 21 starts and nine relief appearances that year. His early success—Bobby won nine of his first 10 decisions—was crucially important to the Yankee cause because Whitey Ford was sidelined with an injury. Shantz, who finished at 11–5, won the league's ERA title with 2.45—on the heels of his 4.35 ERA in 1956.

Following his first Yankee season, Shantz was steadily moved to the bullpen and was used exclusively in relief in 1960. He was the bullpen ace that year, going 5–4 with 11 saves in 42 relief appearances. And Bobby, rather than Bill Mazeroski, might well have been the hero of the seventh game of the 1960 World Series.

With the Pirates leading, 4–0, Bobby took the mound at the start of the third inning and over five innings pitched to the minimum 15 batters (two baserunners were erased on double plays), allowing the Yankees to fight back and go ahead, 7–4. After Gino Cimoli led off the Pirate eighth with a single, Shantz induced Bill Virdon to hit a perfect double-play ball, but the ball took a terrible hop and all hands were safe. The next batter singled and Casey Stengel removed Shantz. The Pirates went on to win, 10–9. It was Bobby's last game as a Yankee.

All-Star
Bobby Shantz was a three-time All-Star. He didn't pitch in the 1951 game as an Athletic or in the 1957 game as a Yankee. But in 1952 (as an Athletic) he fanned the side—Whitey Lockman, Jackie Robinson, and Stan Musial—in his only inning of All-Star work.

Yankee Stats
	W	L	PCT	G	GS	CG	SA	SO	ERA
4 Years	30	18	.625	138	38	14	19	272	2.73
2 World Series	0	1	.000	6	1	0	1	8	4.15
All-Star Games (no appearances)									

BOBBY SHANTZ (Bob Olen)

Career

Frank Joseph O'Shea, born in 1920, brought to the world a freckled face. He was called Speckles, later shortened to Spec. When he got to be a great pitcher, Spec, from Naugatuck, Connecticut, was called the Naugatuck Nugget.

Shea was a versatile ballplayer as a schoolboy, but the advice from his dad, who had been a minor leaguer in Bridgeport, was that a good pitcher stood the best chance of making the majors. So Shea pitched for Naugatuck High School, where Paul Krichell scouted him (once seeing the youngster strike out 22 men in 13 innings) and signed him to a Yankee contract.

The right-hander entered the Yankee farm system in 1940 and pitched there for three seasons. Then came three wartime years in the European theater, where he was badly burned and almost blinded in a gasoline explosion. But Spec survived that nightmare and might have survived Joe McCarthy's final 1946 spring cuts had he not been stricken with appendicitis. McCarthy reluctantly farmed him to Oakland, where Shea went 15–5.

Shea got into great shape for the 1947 spring, made the Yankees, and was the rookie sensation of baseball. He lost his first game, 1–0, even though he three-hit Boston, then peeled off seven consecutive wins. Spec won his first three matchups, two by shutouts, against the Tigers' great Hal Newhouser. Naugatuck went wild, the hometown fans either making the short trip to the Bronx to see him pitch, or listening raptly to radio accounts, and giving Spec a Day at Yankee Stadium. Spec was the league's best pitcher in the season's first half, but was injured much of the second half and went almost two months without a victory. Still, he finished at 14–5 with a 3.07 ERA and 13 completions in 23 starts, then posted two important wins in the seven-game World Series with the Dodgers.

Shea was a great comic, imitator, and mimic—a free-spirited guy who was fun to be around and who was always ready for fun. He captured the imagination of Yankee fans. But while the irreverent Irishman was fun off the field, he was all business on it. His strengths were his cockiness, courage, and poise. He had all the pitches and threw them all with the same delivery. Spud Chandler called the rookie "a finished pitcher."

Shea was constantly battling a weight problem. He put on weight following his great rookie season and, trying to take it off too quickly in the 1948 spring camp, strained his pitching arm. His record slipped to 9–10. The next year he was pitched sparingly in New York and then was sent to the minors. He returned to the Yanks in 1951 and went 5–5 with a bloated 4.33 ERA.

The Yankees traded Shea to Washington early in the 1952 season. Remarkably, Shea resurrected his career with the second-division Senators, going 11–7 in 1952 and 12–7 in 1953. He ended his eight-year big league career in 1955 with an overall mark of 56–46.

All-Star

As a rookie All-Star in 1947, Spec Shea pitched the fourth, fifth, and sixth innings, allowing only one run—a Johnny Mize homer. But the Americans went ahead during Shea's stint and won, 2–1, making Shea the first rookie to win an All-Star Game. The bad news was that Shea's arm stiffened and he was injury-plagued for some time thereafter.

Yankee Stats

	W	L	PCT	G	GS	CG	SA	SO	ERA
4 Years	29	21	.580	100	59	23	3	8	220
1 World Series	2	0	1.000	3	3	1	0	10	2.35
All-Star Games	1	0	1.000	1	0	0	0	2	3.00

SPEC SHEA (NY Yankees)

BILL SKOWRON

Career

In the years following Lou Gehrig's 1939 retirement, the Yankees went through a peck of first basemen, none of them holding the job for more than a few seasons. Not until Bill "Moose" Skowron came along in 1954. After platooning with Joe Collins in 1954–55, Skowron began a seven-season reign at the position in 1956.

At 5'11" and 195 pounds, Skowron, a Chicagoan, was not as big as his nickname suggests. But he was exceptionally strong; he could reach the Yankee Stadium bleachers with a one-handed swing. At Purdue University, Skowron played football (he was a superb punter) and shortstop, hitting .500 in his final collegiate campaign. He was signed by the Yankees and in 1951 broke into pro ball at the age of 21. The next year, at the farm club in Kansas City, Bill hit .341 with a league-leading 31 home runs and 134 RBIs, and was named Minor League Player of the Year. In the minors, Skowron was switched from shortstop to third base and then to first base.

Skowron joined the Yankees in 1954 and in 87 games hit at a staggering .340 average. He followed that with three more .300 seasons in succession. He hit more than 20 homers in four Yankee seasons and collected two pinch-hit grand-slam homers. In 1961, he hit a career-high 28 homers, combining with Roger Maris and Mickey Mantle for 143 roundtrippers. His best all-round season was 1960, when he hit .309 with 34 doubles, 26 homers, and 91 RBIs.

Moose may have been the most successful right-handed hitter at reaching the short right-field porch at Yankee Stadium. Many of his homers were hit the opposite way; his power from center field's 461-foot sign to the right-field line was awesome. Joe DiMaggio and Tony Lazzeri are the only right-handed batters in Yankee history to hit more homers than Skowron.

Moose got the fence-busting hit in the clutch, too. As a perennial World Series performer, Skowron's eight homers ranks seventh on the all-time list. In the seventh game of the 1956 Series, Moose became the sixth man in history to hit a bases-loaded World Series homer, helping the Yanks trounce Brooklyn, 9–0. Two years later his three-run homer in the seventh game wrapped up New York's 6–2 World Series win over Milwaukee and capped the Yanks' great comeback from a three-games-to-one deficit.

BILL SKOWRON (NY Yankees)

Yankee fans loved to coo "Mooooose" much the way they chant "Loooou" these days. Skowron constantly wore a mean-looking scowl, but he was actually a gentle, good-hearted person, who was teased by the locker-room practical jokers and who loved the comradery of the clubhouse. He was one of those guys who helps a club with his clubhouse presence. But he was given to brooding about his hitting in the manner of Charlie Keller.

Injuries kept Skowron from a possible Hall of Fame career. He was repeatedly being hobbled, and persistent back problems greatly reduced his mobility. In only one season (1961) in Moose's 14-year career did he play in as many as 150 games. Moose's bad luck hit rock bottom in 1958–59. Late in 1958 spring training, Skowron hit three grand slams within a week and remained red-hot into the regular season, hitting around .370 in May, when he collapsed with a badly torn back muscle. He was hospitalized for several weeks and finished at .273. The following July, Bill, who was running second in RBIs with 59 (in 74 games), suffered a broken arm, ending his season.

The Yankees traded Skowron to the Los Angeles Dodgers for pitcher Stan Williams in November of 1962. Bill suffered through his worst season in 1963, hitting only .203, and then batted .385 in the Dodgers' World Series sweep of the Yankees. He ended his career in 1967 with 211 home runs and a .282 lifetime average.

All-Star

Bill Skowron's .429 All-Star average is the highest by a Yankee player among those who played in at least three games. He was an All-Star from 1957 through 1961 and made four All-Star starts at first base. He had two hits apiece in the 1957 game and the first game of 1959. He was a combined 2-for-4 in the two 1960 games. He went hitless in the 1958 game and didn't participate in either of the 1961 games.

Yankee Stats

	G	AB	R	H	2B	3B	HR	RBI	BA
9 Years	1,087	3,748	517	1,103	173	44	165	672	.294
7 World Series	35	120	17	34	4	1	7	26	.283
All-Star Games	5	14	1	6	1	0	0	0	.429

SNUFFY STIRNWEISS

Career

George Henry Stirnweiss was born October 26, 1918, the son of a New York City policeman. He learned to play baseball on the sandlots of the Bronx and attended Fordham Prep, then journeyed south to play baseball and football (he was a fine running back) at the University of North Carolina. Stirnweiss never developed into a big man (5'8" and 175 pounds), but he was fast. Snuffy, as he was better known to baseball fans, swiped 73 bases in 83 attempts at Newark in 1942.

Doctors disqualified Stirnweiss from army consideration because of stomach problems and so, in 1943, Snuffy broke in with the Yankees, sharing the shortstop job with Frank Crosetti. Stirnweiss hit a feeble .219, but the next year raised his average exactly 100 points, hitting .319 with 205 hits as New York's regular second baseman.

Over the 1944–45 seasons, Stirnweiss was about the best player in baseball, playing every Yankee game at second base and leading the league in 11 offensive categories. Snuffy won the 1945 batting crown at .309, the lowest league-high average since Elmer Flick hit .306 in 1905. Thus Stirnweiss is in the company of Babe Ruth, Lou Gehrig, Joe DiMaggio, and Mickey Mantle as the only Yankee batting champions.

Stirnweiss was one of the most exciting baserunners in the story of the Yankees. He led the league in 1944 with 55 stolen bases and no Yankee has swiped as many since then. (Snuffy was caught stealing only 11 times that year.) The next year he paced the circuit with 33 stolen bases, the last time a Yankee has led in stolen bases.

Many Yankee stars returned from the service in 1946 and Joe Gordon reassumed his second base job. Manager Joe McCarthy put Snuffy at third, a new position for him. Said McCarthy of the hard-nosed Snuffy: "He's a ballplayer. He can play anywhere. He can play third base with his legs crossed." But Gordon was traded and Stirnweiss returned to second base in 1947–48. His bat had cooled off somewhat, but he was still great in the field. In 1948, he led the league's second sackers in fielding for the second time, his .993 percentage remaining the Yankees' record for second basemen.

Snuffy was a reserve in 1949 and was traded to the St. Louis Browns in 1950. He ended his 10-year big league career in 1952 with a .268 lifetime average and later returned to coach in the Yankee organization.

All-Star
Snuffy Stirnweiss missed out as an All-Star in 1944–45, his best seasons. He was not selected in 1944 and there was no game in 1945. But he was an All-Star third baseman in 1946, delivering a hit and scoring a run in the Americans' 12–0 romp at Fenway Park.

Yankee Stats

	G	AB	R	H	2B	3B	HR	RBI	BA
8 Years	884	3,281	562	899	140	66	27	253	.274
3 World Series	9	28	4	7	0	1	0	3	.250
All-Star Games	1	3	1	1	0	0	0	0	.333

SNUFFY STIRNWEISS

MEL STOTTLEMYRE

Career

Mel Stottlemyre pitched for the Yankees from 1964 through 1974. His tremendous pitching in the closing two months of the 1964 season was the most important factor in the Yankees' winning their 29th pennant (their last until 1976). Without his injury in 1974, the Yankees would have won at least a division title. In between these seasons, the Yankees won nothing. Stottlemyre pitched fantastic ball for mediocre teams. In another Yankee era, Mel would have posted one of the club's great records.

Mel, born in Missouri in 1941, was pitching for Yakima Valley College (Washington) when Yankee scout Eddie Taylor signed him for a small bonus. Mel became part of the Yankee organization in 1961 and was 17–9 the next year at Greensboro. He was 13–3 and had a 1.42 ERA (and would win Minor League Player of the Year honors) at Richmond in August of 1964 when summoned by the third-place Yankees.

In his major league debut on August 12, 1964, Stottlemyre beat Chicago, allowing three runs in a typical effort (his career ERA would be 2.97). Mel later halted a six-game Yankee losing streak, won a game to move the Yankees into first place for good, and pitched a two-hitter on a day when he went 5-for-5 at the plate. Mel finished at 9–3 with a 2.06 ERA and the Yankees finished one game ahead of the White Sox and two ahead of the Orioles. Then Stottlemyre went head-to-head with Bob Gibson in three World Series games. He beat Gibson with a complete-game seven-hitter in Game 2, pitched well but got no decision in Game 5 (Gibson won), and ran out of steam pitching with two days rest in Game 7 (Gibson won).

The Yankees crashed in 1965, but Stottlemyre enjoyed the first of his three 20-win seasons. The next year Mel lost 20 games and became the first American League pitcher since Walter Johnson in 1915–16 to win and lose 20 in consecutive seasons. Mel's 164 wins rank fifth on New York's all-time list. He was a durable workhorse, pitching in at least 250 innings in all nine of his full seasons (1965–73). Twice he led the league in complete games.

Stottlemyre was a rangy, 6'1" right-hander with an exquisite sinkerball. He was not flashy, and in the days before Tommy John converted the groundout to a positive expression, Mel's pitching style was perceived by some as dull. He was an outstanding, efficient,

MEL STOTTLEMYRE (UPI)

hard-working pitcher, but with Tom Seaver striking out hitters by the droves over at Shea Stadium, Mel tended to be overlooked. His was a time of sensational pitchers, and Mel blended into the background. When Mel posted his career-high 21 wins in 1968, Denny McLain was winning 31. Mel was good all the same. His 40 lifetime shutouts ties Sandy Koufax and is only five behind the total of all-time Yankee leader Whitey Ford.

In 1974, Mel ended a streak of 272 consecutive starts, going back to April of 1967, with a relief appearance. Shortly thereafter, with a torn rotator cuff in his pitching shoulder and a record of 6–7, Stottlemyre was lost for the year. His attempted comeback the following spring was aborted when Gabe Paul released him. The last member of the 1964 Yankees was gone from the scene.

All-Star

Mel Stottlemyre was a five-time All-Star, making the team in 1965–66 and 1968–70. He turned in excellent relief efforts in 1966, 1968, and 1970. He pitched two shutout innings in the 1966 game, faced one batter and fanned Hank Aaron in the 1968 game, and hurled a perfect 1 2/3 innings in the 1970 game (striking out Pete Rose in the process).

Stottlemyre started and pitched two innings of the 1969 game, played at Robert F. Kennedy Stadium in Washington. (Mel is the last Yankee pitcher to open an All-Star Game.) He gave up an unearned first-inning run, then was touched for a two-run second-inning homer by Johnny Bench. Mel took the defeat, and the Nationals went on to a 9–3 triumph.

Yankee Stats

	W	L	PCT	G	GS	CG	SA	SO	ERA
11 Years	164	139	.541	360	356	152	1	1,257	2.97
1 World Series	1	1	.500	3	3	1	0	12	3.15
All-Star Games	0	1	.000	4	1	0	0	4	3.00

RALPH TERRY

Career

Ralph Terry was on his way to being remembered for his World Series failures. It was Terry who lost two games in the 1960 Series and allowed Bill Mazeroski's Series-winning homer. It was Terry who suffered New York's only defeat in the 1961 Series, and it was Terry who lost Game 2 of the 1962 Series against San Francisco. But it was also Terry who came back in Game 5 of that Series to pitch a gutty 5–3 victory. And it was Terry who, given the ball for the winner-takes-all seventh game at Candlestick Park, pitched one of the greatest pressure games in history. Going the route, Terry allowed only four hits, walked none, and escaped a messy ninth-inning jam to win, 1–0. "I want to thank God for a second opportunity," said Ralph. "You don't often get a second chance to prove yourself, in baseball or in life."

The 6′3″ native of Big Cabin, Oklahoma, was the subject of a dispute between the Yankees and Cardinals, both clubs arguing they had Ralph under contract. Commissioner Frick ruled in favor of the Yankees and the 18-year-old Terry broke in with Binghamton in 1954, winning 11 games. Ralph was 13–4 in Denver in 1956 and in his major league debut on August 6, 1956, beat Boston. He was traded in June of 1957 to the Kansas City A's, where he picked up valuable experience, and the Yankees got him back two years later. Late in the 1960 season, he started gaining consistency, finishing at 10–8 and winning the pennant clincher. He came into his own with a 16–3 record in 1961.

As a young major leaguer, Terry was sometimes accused of experimenting with his pitches too much. But his career skyrocketed in 1961 when Johnny Sain taught him the slider, which became Ralph's "out pitch"—his meal ticket—and he mixed it beautifully with his rising fastball and changeup curveball. He was an efficient fast worker and had great control.

Terry posted a 23–12 record in 1962 and led the league in wins, games started (39), and innings pitched (299). No Yankee right-hander had won as many games since George Pipgras won 24 in 1928. Ralph set a Yankee record by allowing 40 home runs, but since he walked fewer than two men per nine innings, most of them were solo jobs. Then came his great World Series, Terry's finest hour.

Terry was a hardluck 17–15 in 1963. His ERA only went up to 3.22 (from 3.19 in 1962), but he received little support and lost nine one-run games. Ralph suffered from lack of work in 1964, slumped to 7–11, and was traded to the Indians after the season. At age 31, he finished his career with the Mets in 1967, the winner of 107 big league games.

All-Star
Ralph Terry was an All-Star in 1962, a year when two games were played. The American League used seven different pitchers in the two games, but Ralph wasn't one of them.

Yankee Stats

	W	L	PCT	G	GS	CG	SA	SO	ERA
8 Years	78	59	.569	210	161	56	8	615	3.44
5 World Series	2	4	.333	9	6	2	0	31	2.93

All-Star Games (no appearances)

RALPH TERRY (NY Yankees)

Career

Born September 20, 1937, in Detroit, Tom Tresh was the son of Mike Tresh, a one-time catcher for the White Sox (1938–48) and the Indians (1949). Tom broke into the Yankee organization in 1958, making several stops. At Richmond, the Yanks' top farm club, he hit .315 in 1961; that year he got into nine Yankee games.

The Yankees were in a bind in the spring of 1962. Shortstop Tony Kubek was in the army and Manager Ralph Houk let Tresh and Phil Linz battle for the job. Both were excellent and both made the club, but Tresh won the starting berth. When Kubek returned in August, Houk switched Tresh to left field, where Tom was sensational, although he hadn't played there since he was a kid. Tresh finished the year with 20 homers, 93 RBIs, 94 runs scored, and a .286 average, and won the league's Rookie of the Year Award. He then shone in the World Series against San Francisco, hitting .321, winning Game 5 with an eighth-inning three-run homer, and saving a 1–0 Yankee win in Game 7 by robbing Willie Mays of a hit just prior to a Willie McCovey triple.

Tresh, who like Mickey Mantle was a switch hitter and was fast (although he didn't have Mantle's blazing speed), had a better rookie year than Mantle had in 1951. But he was prematurely labeled "the next Mickey Mantle." Tresh idolized Mantle (and would later name a son after Mickey), but although he was a fine all-round player, he was not in Mickey's class.

Tresh was, however, one of the best power hitters in the American League. Four times he hit more than 20 homers, with a high of 27 in 1966. Three times Tom hit homers from both sides of the plate in the same game, joining Mantle (who did it 10 times) as the second Yankee to accomplish that ambidextrous feat. In 1965, Tresh's best all-round season, he put on two great performances against Chicago at Yankee Stadium. In one game, he hit three consecutive homers and then lined a single. In another, Tom leaped into the left-field seats to steal a homer with two outs in the 10th inning and then led off the bottom half with a four-bagger to win it.

Tresh was an excellent outfielder and had the speed needed to cover the bulging left side of the left-fielder's position at Yankee Stadium. He fielded 64 games at third base in 1966 and returned to shortstop in 1968.

After his fine 1965 season, Tresh, a quiet, noncontroversial person, was struck with a succession of disabling injuries and his career suffered. Starting with his .279 average in 1965, Tresh slipped to .233 to .219 to .195. He was hitting .182 when New York traded him to Detroit in June of 1969, Tresh's last big league season.

All-Star

Tom Tresh was selected to the American League's All-Star roster as a shortstop in 1962 and as an outfielder in 1963. He didn't play in the first game of 1962. But in that year's second game, which the Americans won, 9–4, at Wrigley Field, Tresh had a double and an RBI in two trips. He played center field but didn't bat in the 1963 game.

Yankee Stats

	B	AB	R	H	2B	3B	HR	RBI	BA
9 Years	1,098	3,920	549	967	166	33	140	493	.247
3 World Series	18	65	10	18	3	0	4	13	.277
All-Star Games	2	2	0	1	1	0	0	1	.500

TOM TRESH

BOB TURLEY

Career

Talented major league pitchers, especially those falling a notch or two below Hall of Fame caliber, dream of putting everything together for one season and having their names spoken in the same breath with the Mathewsons and Groves and Fords. Bullet Bob Turley, who won 101 major league games, experienced such a season; in 1958, at 21–7, he was baseball's best pitcher, the winner of the Cy Young Award (which in 1958 was given to the best pitcher in the majors). Bob led the American League in both wins and winning percentage (.750) and in completed games (19) while making only 31 starts.

But what really made Turley's 1958 so special was his World Series performance—two wins and a save in the final three games—in New York's comeback victory from a three-games-to-one deficit. After Milwaukee kayoed him in the first inning of the second game, Turley returned in the fifth game to pitch a five-hit shutout with 10 strikeouts. In the sixth game, Turley got the last out with the tying run on third and the winning run on first. In the seventh game, Bob pitched the final 6 2/3 innings, allowing only two hits and one run, and got credit for the Yankees' 6–2 victory.

The native of Troy, Illinois, began his pitching career by throwing pears in his backyard. Bullet Bob began with the St. Louis Browns' organization and reached the Browns in 1951. Three years later the Browns moved to Baltimore and the 24-year-old Turley won 14 games for the seventh-place Orioles. The Yankees acquired Turley as part of an 18-player transaction late in 1954. In his first three seasons in New York, Bob went 17–13, 8–4, and 13–6.

Bullet Bob came by his name honestly. The burly, 215-pound right-hander, who didn't even use a full windup, could hum a fastball with the best of them. He allowed only 7.18 hits per nine innings in his career, a ratio that ranks among the top 10 in history, and as a Yankee he pitched three one-hitters. When Turley fanned 210 batters and walked 177 in 1955, it was the most strikeouts by a Yankee pitcher in 51 years and the most walks ever by a Yankee right-hander. Turley's fastball was officially clocked in 1960 (well past his prime as a hard thrower) at 90.7 mph. In his career, Bullet Bob fanned at least 10 men in 17 games. A batsman who was hit had the dubious pleasure of knowing that Bob didn't mean it—Bob would not deliberately aim at the batter. He was just too nice a guy for brushback pitching.

Turley was a combined 17–14 over the 1959–60 seasons. He suffered from a sore arm in 1961, attempted to pitch through the pain, but finally had to be shelved for the season. He had postseason surgery, but was unable to reclaim his former form. His career ended with the Angels and Red Sox in 1963.

All-Star

Bob Turley, who made the All-Stars as an Oriole in 1954, was a Yankee All-Star in 1955 and 1958. He didn't pitch in 1955, but got the starting nod in the 1958 game played in Baltimore. Turley allowed three early runs, but the rest of the staff blanked the Nationals and the Americans won, 4–3.

Yankee Stats

	W	L	PCT	G	GS	CG	SA	SO	ERA
8 Years	82	52	.612	234	175	58	12	909	3.62
5 World Series	4	3	.571	15	8	3	1	46	3.19
All-Star Games	0	0	.000	1	1	0	0	0	16.17

BOB TURLEY (UPI)

Career

The Yankees signed Roy White in 1961, at the height of their dynasty. White joined the team in 1965, the year the dynasty came tumbling down. White was there for the entire dry spell (1965–75) and anguished with the fans, who had only White, Bobby Murcer (and later Thurman Munson) to cheer about. It was only when the Yankees won three pennants in a row (1976–78) that Roy was fully appreciated for his solid, steady play, as a player in the mold of Tommy Henrich and Hank Bauer. And as Roy closed out his 15-year Yankee career in 1979, the fans showed their appreciation by constantly showering him with applause.

Roy White was born December 27, 1943, in Los Angeles and grew up on the tough streets of Compton, California. He overcame a childhood bout with polio, but most scouts regarded him as too small (he grew to 5'10" and 165 pounds). Except Yankee scout Tuffy Hashem, who signed White. Roy spent four seasons as a minor league second baseman. He was the Southern League's MVP (at Columbus, Georgia) in 1965, and in 14 games with the Yankees he hit .333.

Johnny Keane, Roy's first Yankee manager, told White he had a chance of being another Curt Flood, and in the spring of 1966 shifted Roy from second base to the outfield. But Roy put too much pressure on himself, didn't field well, and hit only .225 in 115 games. The next year he hit .343 on loan to the Dodgers' Spokane team, then returned to New York to hit .224.

In 1968, White proved he could hit big league pitching and became the Yankees' left fielder, a job he held through 1977. Twice Roy played in all 162 games. He became a top-fielding left fielder (he fielded 1.000 in 145 games in 1971), seldom misplaying a ball and almost always throwing to the right base. He timed his leaps perfectly in making over-the-fence catches. His only deficiency as a ballplayer was a weak throwing arm.

White, the second-best switch hitter (behind Mantle) in Yankee history, was a slashing line-drive hitter to all fields. He switch-hit homers in the same game five times, once switch-hit triples in the same game, and twice had five-hit games. His best season was 1970, when he hit .296 with 22 homers, 94 RBIs, and 109 runs scored. Scoring runs was a White trademark; he scored more than

ROY WHITE (NY Yankees)

80 runs in six seasons and led the league with 104 in 1976. One reason he scored so often was his exceptional batting eye; he ranks fourth on New York's all-time walk list.

White had the speed to bat leadoff, the bat control to bat second, and the hitting talent to bat third. There was even a time when White batted cleanup on a regular basis for the Yanks. He did the important moving-up-the-runner tasks well, such as bunting, hitting behind the runner, executing the hit-and-run play, and hitting the sacrifice fly. In 1971 he set a league record with 17 sacrifice flies. And Roy was excellent on the basepaths, stealing 232 bases to rank second in Yankee history.

White delivered the most important hit of the 1977 season. In late June, the Red Sox charged into Yankee Stadium, leading the Yankees by four games. Boston led, 5–3, when, with two out in the ninth inning, White blasted a two-run homer. New York won in extra innings, swept the series, and climbed back into the race.

The Yankees went on to win the World Series in 1977. But White watched most of the postseason action from the bench and hardly felt like celebrating. It was a different story in 1978, when Roy hit safely in all of New York's 11 postseason games. He celebrated that World Series victory with gusto.

On and off the field, White conducted himself with class. Roy also shed his street-kid life and became a gentleman of sophisticated tastes, who was well read and who explored the cultural advantages of New York City, as he would later explore oriental cultures as a player in Japan.

Following a part-time role in 1979, White left the Yankees and enjoyed three fine seasons playing in the Japanese big leagues. In 1983, Roy returned to the Yankees as a coach, pleasing everyone.

All-Star

Roy White was an All-Star in 1969 and 1970. He struck out as a pinch hitter in the 1969 game and didn't get into the 1970 game.

Yankee Stats

	G	AB	R	H	2B	3B	HR	RBI	BA
15 Years	1,881	6,650	964	1,803	300	51	160	758	.271
3 Champ. Series	13	38	11	12	6	0	1	4	.316
3 World Series	12	41	9	10	0	0	1	4	.244
All-Star Games	1	1	0	0	0	0	0	0	.000

DAVE WINFIELD

Career

Dave Winfield may be one of the greatest all-round athletes to have come into the major leagues. He was drafted by three professional sports—major league baseball, professional basketball (by both the NBA and the erstwhile ABA), and professional football—after a spectacular athletic career at the University of Minnesota. Dave, who was made a 1973 first-round draft choice by the San Diego Padres, leaped right to the majors from the Minnesota campus and hit safely in his first six games. He had several big years for the Padres.

In December of 1980, the Yankees signed free-agent Winfield to a 10-year multi-million dollar contract that pushed the 29-year-old Dave to the head of the class in player salaries. The 6'6", 220-pounder from St. Paul, Minnesota,was hitting .324 when the players' strike began in June of 1981. He finished the year as New York's club leader in a majority of batting categories.

In 1981, Winfield brought a brand of excellence in all-round skills not seen on a New York baseball diamond in some time. He rapped smoking line drives to all fields and hit a 475-foot homer down the left-field ambulance runway at Yankee Stadium. On the bases, he turned normal singles into doubles with seven or eight giant strides, loping into second base. At the Stadium, he would steal home runs out of the left-field stands or play the rebound perfectly in the corner and rifle a bullet to second base to nail a hitter who believed he had a "sure" double.

But Winfield slumped in the 1981 postseason. He hit .350 against Milwaukee, but then hit .154 against Oakland and finally .045 against Los Angeles in the World Series. The following spring the experts wondered whether Winfield could rebound from his poor World Series and whether he could replace the departed Reggie Jackson as New York's star. He did both.

In 1982 the confident Winfield proved what a great player he is, hitting .280 with 37 homers and 106 RBIs, winning a Gold Glove, and leading league outfielders with 17 assists. Eleven of his homers were hit in September, when Dave was named the American League Player of the Month. In Yankee history, only Joe DiMaggio has hit more homers in a season as a right-handed hitter.

Winfield has become a hero to a lot of kids. He donates a good portion of his time and money to his foundation that helps disadvantaged kids. Dave works with youth groups, sets up scholarship programs, and hosts kids at ball games, among other things.

All-Star
Dave Winfield has played in six consecutive All-Star Games, 1977–82. As a Padre, he represented the National League in four games. Overall, Dave is a .294 hitter (5-for-17).

In 1981, Winfield gained a starting berth and went hitless in four trips. Dave finished fourth among outfielders in the 1982 voting, coming in only about 3,000 votes behind Fred Lynn. He was named to the team and delivered a single in two at bats.

Yankee Stats

	G	AB	R	H	2B	3B	HR	RBI	BA
2 Years	245	927	136	265	49	9	50	174	.286
1 Champ. Series	3	13	2	2	1	0	0	2	.154
1 World Series	6	22	0	1	0	0	0	1	.045
All-Star Games	2	6	0	1	0	0	0	0	.167

DAVE WINFIELD

NEW YORK YANKEE ALL-STAR GAME HIGHLIGHTS

1933 Game
At Comiskey Park, Chicago
AL 4, NL 2.
Babe Ruth hits a two-run homer, the first four-bagger in All-Star history. Lefty Gomez starts, gets credit for the win, and knocks in the first run in All-Star history.

1934 Game
At the Polo Grounds, New York
AL 9, NL 7.
Bill Dickey singles off Carl Hubbell, snapping King Carl's strikeout string of five great hitters—Babe Ruth, Lou Gehrig, Jimmie Foxx, Al Simmons, and Joe Cronin.

1935 Game
At Municipal Stadium, Cleveland
AL 4, NL 1.
Lefty Gomez starts and pitches six strong innings to gain the victory. The National League has the rules changed shortly thereafter so that no one pitcher can go more than three innings in a regulation All-Star Game.

1936 Game
At Braves Field, Boston
NL 4, AL 3.
Lou Gehrig hits a seventh-inning home run off Curt Davis, and Joe McCarthy loses his All-Star managerial debut. (Marse Joe is substituting for the ill Mickey Cochrane.)

1937 Game
At Griffith Stadium, Washington, D.C.
AL 8, NL 3.
Lefty Gomez is the starter and winner for the third time, and Lou Gehrig, who homers and doubles, knocks in four runs.

1938 Game
At Crosley Field, Cincinnati
NL 4, AL 1.
Joe DiMaggio singles and scores his team's lone run, and starter Lefty Gomez suffers his only All-Star defeat.

1939 Game
At Yankee Stadium, New York
AL 3, NL 1.
Joe DiMaggio hits a solo homer and Red Ruffing makes the start. Joe McCarthy also starts Red Rolfe, Bill Dickey, George Selkirk, and Joe Gordon, six Yankees in all.

1940 Game
At Sportsman's Park, St. Louis
NL 4, AL 0.
Red Ruffing gets the starting nod, goes three innings, and suffers the defeat.

1941 Game
At Briggs Stadium, Detroit
AL 7, NL 5.
Joe DiMaggio has a double, knocks in a run, and scores three runs. DiMaggio and Joe Gordon are on base when Ted Williams hits a game-winning homer in the bottom of the ninth inning.

1942 Game
At the Polo Grounds, New York
AL 3, NL 1.
Spud Chandler starts, pitches four shutout innings, and receives the victory. Joe DiMaggio raps two hits.

1943 Game
At Shibe Park, Philadelphia
AL 5, NL 3.
Manager Joe McCarthy doesn't use a single one of his six Yankee All-Stars, apparently because he is stung by criticism that he favors his own players in the summer exhibition. Marse Joe wins anyway.

1944 Game
At Forbes Field, Pittsburgh
NL 7, AL 1.
Hank Borowy opens the contest with three shutout innings and drives in his team's only run of the day.

1945 Game
Cancelled because of wartime curtailment on travel.

1946 Game
At Fenway Park, Boston
AL 12, NL 0.
Charlie Keller gets the American League off and running with a two-run first-inning homer. Joe Gordon later knocks in a pair of runs.

1947 Game
At Wrigley Field, Chicago
AL 2, NL 1.
Spec Shea allows only one run over the three middle innings and becomes the first rookie to win in All-Star history. Joe Page shuts the door and gains a save.

1948 Game
At Sportsman's Park, St. Louis
AL 5, NL 2.
Vic Raschi blanks the National League over the middle three innings, gains the win, and knocks in two runs with a single. George McQuinn has two hits, scores a run, and steals a base.

1949 Game
At Ebbets Field, Brooklyn
AL 11, NL 7.
Vic Raschi is the American League's only effective pitcher. He pitches the final three innings without allowing a run and gets credit for a save. Joe DiMaggio has two hits and knocks in three runs.

1950 Game
At Comiskey Park, Chicago
NL 4, AL 3 (14 innings).
Vic Raschi is the starter, Phil Rizzuto cracks a pair of hits, and Casey Stengel loses his All-Star debut.

1951 Game
At Briggs Stadium, Detroit
NL 8, AL 3.
Joe DiMaggio is a member of the All-Star team for the last time, but a leg injury prevents him from playing.

1952 Game
At Shibe Park, Philadelphia
NL 3, AL 2 (5 innings—rain shortened).
Vic Raschi is the starting pitcher and Hank Bauer manages one of the five hits made by the American League.

1953 Game
At Crosley Field, Cincinnati
NL 5, AL 1.
Johnny Mize delivers a ninth-inning pinch-hit single, but it isn't enough and Allie Reynolds takes the loss.

1954 Game
At Municipal Stadium, Cleveland
AL 11, NL 9.
Manager Casey Stengel snaps a four-game All-Star losing streak. Whitey Ford opens and pitches three shutout innings. Yogi Berra and Mickey Mantle each stroke a pair of hits and score a total of three runs.

1955 Game
At County Stadium, Milwaukee
NL 6, AL 5 (12 innings).
Mickey Mantle has two hits, including a 430-foot homer off Robin Roberts that is good for three runs.

1956 Game
At Griffith Stadium, Washington, D.C.
NL 7, AL 3.
Mickey Mantle belts a home run off Warren Spahn and Yogi Berra has a perfect 2-for-2 day.

1957 Game
At Busch Stadium, St. Louis
AL 6, NL 5.
Bob Grim comes in to record the final out of the game and earn a save. Bill Skowron has a double and single, and scores a run.

1958 Game
At Memorial Stadium, Baltimore
AL 4, NL 3.
Gil McDougald delivers a sixth-inning pinch-hit single to knock in the winning run. Bob Turley makes the start and is roughed up.

1959 First Game
At Forbes Field, Pittsburgh
NL 5, AL 4.
Ryne Duren allows only one hit and strikes out four over the middle three innings, but Whitey Ford takes the loss. Bill Skowron contributes a pair of safeties.

1959 Second Game
At Memorial Coliseum, Los Angeles
AL 5, NL 3.
Manager Casey Stengel is victorious in his final All-Star appearance. Yogi Berra wallops a long two-run homer off Don Drysdale in the third inning.

1960 First Game
At Municipal Stadium, Kansas City
NL 5, AL 3.
Jim Coates pitches two shutout innings in relief and Bill Skowron gets one of the six hits made by the American League.

1960 Second Game
At Yankee Stadium, New York
NL 6, AL 0.
Whitey Ford makes the start, allows three runs in three innings, and absorbs the loss. Mickey Mantle and Bill Skowron have one hit apiece.

1961 First Game
At Candlestick Park, San Francisco
NL 5, AL 4 (10 innings).
Whitey Ford opens and pitches three strong innings. Roger Maris makes one of the four hits made by the American League.

1961 Second Game
At Fenway Park, Boston
AL 1, NL 1 (rain stops play after 9 innings).
Mickey Mantle, Elston Howard, and Roger Maris are a combined 0-for-6, and the American League is held to four hits.

1962 First Game
At D.C. Stadium, Washington, D.C.
NL 3, AL 1.
Roger Maris knocks in the American League's only run in the sixth inning with a long sacrifice fly to the wall in right-center field.

1962 Second Game
At Wrigley Field, Chicago
AL 9, NL 4.
Roger Maris has a big day as he doubles, knocks in a run, and scores twice. Tom Tresh also doubles and drives in a run.

1963 Game
At Municipal Stadium, Cleveland
NL 5, AL 3.
Jim Bouton pitches one perfect inning in relief, but Yankee hitters go a combined 0-for-7 at the plate.

1964 Game
At Shea Stadium, New York
NL 7, AL 4.
Mickey Mantle and Bobby Richardson each make one hit, and Mantle and Elston Howard each score once.

1965 Game
At Metropolitan Stadium, Bloomington, Minnesota
NL 6, AL 5.
Bobby Richardson and Joe Pepitone are the only Yankees to play. They are a combined 0-for-3 at the plate.

1966 Game
At Busch Memorial Stadium, St. Louis
NL 2, AL 1 (10 innings).
Mel Stottlemyre blanks the National League over the sixth and seventh innings, allowing only one hit.

1967 Game

At Anaheim Stadium, Anaheim, California
NL 2, AL 1 (15 innings).
Al Downing blanks the National League over the ninth and tenth innings, striking out Roberto Clemente and Richie Allen.

1968 Game

At Astrodome, Houston
NL 1, AL 0.
Mickey Mantle, playing in his final All-Star Game, receives the day's biggest cheers. He pinch-hits in the eighth inning, but becomes one of Tom Seaver's five strikeout victims.

1969 Game

At Robert F. Kennedy Stadium, Washington, D.C.
NL 9, AL 3.
Mel Stottlemyre is the starting and losing pitcher, allowing three runs (two earned) in two innings.

1970 Game

At Riverfront Stadium, Cincinnati
NL 5, AL 4 (12 innings).
Mel Stottlemyre is flawless in recording five outs as a late-inning relief pitcher.

1971 Game

At Tiger Stadium, Detroit
AL 6, NL 4.
Bobby Murcer makes one hit in three at bats and the American League snaps an eight-game losing streak in All-Star competition.

1972 Game

At Atlanta Stadium, Atlanta
NL 4, AL 3 (10 innings).
Bobby Murcer is the only Yankee to take part, starting in center field and going hitless in three trips.

1973 Game

At Royals Stadium, Kansas City
NL 7, AL 1.
Sparky Lyle pitches one scoreless inning in relief and strikes out Willie Mays in Mays' final All-Star at bat.

1974 Game
At Three Rivers Stadium, Pittsburgh
NL 7, AL 2.
Thurman Munson doubles and scores one of his team's two runs.

1975 Game
At County Stadium, Milwaukee
NL 6, AL 3.
Catfish Hunter gets cuffed around in late-inning relief and takes the defeat. Thurman Munson and Graig Nettles each make one hit and Nettles steals a base.

1976 Game
At Veterans Stadium, Philadelphia
NL 7, AL 1.
Catfish Hunter, Thurman Munson, Chris Chambliss, and Mickey Rivers all play with limited success, although Rivers gets one hit.

1977 Game
At Yankee Stadium, New York
NL 7, AL 5.
Billy Martin is the first Yankee manager to pilot an All-Star team since Ralph Houk in 1963. Reggie Jackson and Willie Randolph each produce one hit, with Willie knocking in a run.

1978 Game
At San Diego Stadium, San Diego
NL 7, AL 3.
Ron Guidry pitches to one batter and records the final out of the seventh inning, keeping the game tied. Rich Gossage is roughed up in the eighth and takes the loss.

1979 Game
At Kingdome, Seattle
NL 7, AL 6.
Graig Nettles enters the game as a defensive replacement for George Brett and gets a hit in his only at bat.

1980 Game
At Dodger Stadium, Los Angeles
NL 4, AL 2.
Tommy John suffers the loss. Willie Randolph has a hit in three at bats.

1981 Game
At Municipal Stadium, Cleveland
NL 5, AL 4.
Bucky Dent has a double and single in two at bats.

1982 Game
At Olympic Stadium, Montreal
NL 4, AL 1.
Dave Winfield is the only Yankee to play, and he gets one hit in two trips.